African Institutions

African Institutions

Challenges to Political, Social, and Economic Foundations of Africa's Development

Ali A. Mazrui and Francis Wiafe-Amoako

ROWMAN & LITTLEFIELD
Lanham • Boulder • New York • London

Published by Rowman & Littlefield
A wholly owned subsidiary of The Rowman & Littlefield Publishing Group, Inc.
4501 Forbes Boulevard, Suite 200, Lanham, Maryland 20706
www.rowman.com

Unit A, Whitacre Mews, 26-34 Stannary Street, London SE11 4AB

British Library Cataloguing in Publication Information Available

Library of Congress Cataloging-in-Publication Data

Mazrui, Ali A.
African institutions : Challenges to political, social, and economic foundations of Africa's development / by Ali A. Mazrui and Francis Wiafe-Amoako.
p. cm.
Includes bibliographical references and index.
ISBN 978-1-4422-3952-4 (cloth : alk. paper) -- ISBN 978-1-4422-3953-1 (pbk. : alk. paper) -- ISBN 978-1-4422-3954-8 (electronic)
1. Economic development--Political aspects--Africa. 2. Economic development--Social aspects--Africa. 3. Social institutions--Africa. 4. Democratization--Africa. 5. Political stability--Africa. 6 Legitimacy of governments--Africa. I. Wiafe-Amoako, Francis, author. II. Title.
JQ1875.M393 2015
320.96--dc23
2016023819

∞ ™ The paper used in this publication meets the minimum requirements of American National Standard for Information Sciences Permanence of Paper for Printed Library Materials, ANSI/NISO Z39.48-1992.

Printed in the United States of America

In memory of
Professor Ali A. Mazrui

And
My wife
Agnes Wiafe-Amoako

Contents

Preface

Challenges to Africa's development lie primarily in its domestic institutions. Effective strategies by the international community and international development organizations to confront development challenges are fundamental steps to deal with the situation. However, contemporary institutions as they exist on the African continent are sometimes incompatible with domestic realities. The book raises the realities of traditional/contemporary institutional dilemmas to any meaningful effort at political, social, and economic development as well as democratic consolidation in Africa.

Every political system, either developed or adopted, has consequences on the structure of the society and the level of development. It is for this reason that the primary objective of this book is to take a look at institutions and their effect on Africa's development. The nature of Africa's political institutions challenges the democracy as conceptualized and practiced in the West. This book aims to provide a significant contribution to the discourses of the democratization process and development in Africa. Much of the concerns of instability in Africa have been associated with the lack of democratic consolidation in the region. The book discusses the challenges of democratization in Africa in a unique way. It argues that democracy and development in Africa face tremendous challenges as a result of the existing institutions. Among the significant issues discussed are historical and colonial realities that hinder democracy, what role legitimacy play in the democratic process, the relationship between natural resource and the democratic process, ideology and effect on Africa's politics and economy, ethnicity and Africa's constitutions, and gender and politics in Africa.

This book emphasizes the fact that no pragmatic discussion on Africa's development could be achieved without addressing institutional challenges. These challenges are not limited to whether or not Africa should adapt some foreign institutions; but one that has substantial roots in domestic norms that define the nature of the society itself. The institutional challenges in some cases have to do with the incompatibility of foreign and domestic institutions. Thus, the fundamental issue is to understand African societies- its culture, and other dynamics that have sustained Africa's society in the past.

This book could not have come at an appropriate time where international development projects in Africa is at the top of the agenda of donors both public and private. This is also the time that accountability is at the highest and donors seek to evaluate the real impact of every dollar spent. The book redirects the attention of policymakers, practitioners, and donors to some institutional building blocks, and also provides the research community with some explanations of underdevelopment in Africa.

Acknowledgments

I would like to thank my family, especially my wife Agnes Wiafe-Amoako for her support in taking care of the children while I was away as a visiting assistant professor at the college Wooster in Ohio. At Wooster I had some quality time to reflect on the manuscript and to complete it. Our children Stephen, Francisca, and Aneesah have been a source of inspiration to me, and this inspiration always encourages me to move to a higher height. Many thanks also go to my brother-in-law Dr. Stephen Maxwell Donkor for his invaluable support and encouragement.

I thank the College of Wooster for providing me with some support from the faculty development fund in the final write-up. I also want to acknowledge my two research assistants Mohammed Sarhan and Joon (Peter) Hyuk Lee for providing data collection and writing assistance.

I also acknowledge the Institute for Global Cultural Studies for coordinating the chapters contributed by Professor Ali A. Mazrui and making this book a reality.

ONE

Institutions

An Introduction

Francis Wiafe-Amoako

"Africa does not need strong men; it needs strong institutions."
—U.S. President Barack H. Obama in Ghana
on his first trip to Africa in 2009

Underlying state stability, security, and development are institutional canons. The consolidation of Africa's democracy and development is not an exception. Institutions[1] have been an instrumental part of societal life, be it politics, economy, justice systems, and the like. This is because laws and rules shape behavior patterns, and ensure transparency, predictability, and structure expectation. Irrespective of what institutions are put in place, once adopted, the challenge now becomes how those institutions will meet people's expectation.

Thus, the relevance of institutions is anchored more in their extrinsic value than their intrinsic value. Having institutions in place, though necessary, is not sufficient to legitimize those institutions. The intrinsic value of institutions may be useful in the short term. The real test comes in the long term. Progressive-minded elites and policy makers need to look out for the reduction of relevance of institutions and make adjustments for change.

Within the international arena, the United Nations has been an instrumental institution that has served the needs of states post-1945. Through

1

the UN system, interstate conflicts have waned and collaborative efforts have been put in place to deal with global problems. The Preamble of the Charter of the United Nations states:

WE THE PEOPLES OF THE UNITED NATIONS DETERMINED:

- to save succeeding generations from the scourge of war, which twice in our lifetime has brought untold sorrow to mankind, and
- to reaffirm faith in fundamental human rights, in the dignity and worth of the human person, in the equal rights of men and women and of nations large and small, and
- to establish conditions under which justice and respect for the obligations arising from treaties and other sources of international law can be maintained, and
- to promote social progress and better standards of life in larger freedom,

AND FOR THESE ENDS:

- to practice tolerance and live together in peace with one another as good neighbors, and
- to unite our strength to maintain international peace and security, and
- to ensure, by the acceptance of principles and the institution of methods, that armed force shall not be used, save in the common interest, and
- to employ international machinery for the promotion of the economic and social advancement of all peoples.

After two successive wars (World War I and World War II), the preamble to the UN Charter structured states' expectations after they have signed off on it. The inability of the League of Nations to deliver the expectations stipulated in its articles could explain why it was completely set aside for a new institution—the United Nations. All of the 19 chapters and 111 articles in the UN Charter provided a new way forward in the post-1945 world order.

Though the Cold War interrupted states' expectations of the United Nations for about four decades, the United Nations as an institution has held its own. It has mobilized global efforts to solve global problems such as reducing interstate conflicts, encouraging diplomacy, enhancing human rights, and dealing with issues of the environment, to mention a few. However, contemporary events have led to some states (the United States and other emerging economies) questioning the relevance of the United Nations as an institution in the twenty-first century. The Security Council basically serves the needs of its five permanent members—China, France, Russia Federation, the United Kingdom, and the United States.

Some of the ways that the United Nations has tried to remain relevant is to collaborate with regional organizations such as the North Atlantic Treaty Organization (NATO) and the African Union (AU). NATO is now becoming the substantive military wing of the United Nations, and NATO states such as Germany relish their newfound role of carving their own influence in the global security arena. In Africa, the United Nations has collaborated with the AU to create the African Union Mission in Somalia (AMISOM), which is a regional peacekeeping mission created in 2007. Established by the United Nations and working in collaboration with the African Union, the AU-UN mission in Darfur (UNAMID) is also a hybrid peacekeeping operation in that region of Sudan. Thus the United Nations, by working with regional organizations, is rebranding itself and incorporating some realities within the contemporary world order into its operations.

The discussions in this book examine the nature of Africa's institutions and the effect of those institutions on democratic consolidation. There is no doubt that the instability of the state systems in Africa has profound effects on the continent's domestic development and competition in the international arena. The fragility of the state in Africa goes beyond colonial institutional legacies. As Claude Ake argued (1996), fundamental institutional pillars have not been considered in Africa's political and economic life since independence. Thus this book sets out to discuss fundamental institutional issues in relation to Africa's stability, security, and development. It identifies areas of institutional challenges that need to receive utmost attention if the perennial security, stability, and development challenges on the continent are to be addressed.

REVIEWING INSTITUTIONS AND IMPLICATION FOR AFRICA

The nature of institutions has scholars trying to unpack what actually is an institution's role in society. While some have viewed institutions as shaping behaviors, others have discussed institutions as a constraint on behavior. However, both of these perspectives regarding institutions demonstrate the influential nature of institutions.

Douglas North describes institutions as "the humanly devised constraints that structure political, economic, and social interactions. Institutions consist of both informal constraints (sanctions, taboos, customs, traditions, and codes of conduct) and formal rules (constitutions, laws, and property rights)" (North, 1991, p. 97).[2] Though North views institutions as constraints, he does however note that societies create institutions (formal and informal) to ensure the reduction of uncertainties in day-to-day interactions—which he refers to as "exchange." North's discussion of institutions within an economic setting has significant implications for politics and society. He notes that institutions, though a constraint, define set choices that people engaged in constant interactions have. The relevance of North's argument cannot be overemphasized in contemporary democratization in Africa and African society.

Africa's political system has evolved. After tinkering with single-party rule interspersed with military regimes, African states have settled for a transition to democracy in the post-1990 era. However, the democratization process is far from over. Democracy and its practice in Africa is viewed suspiciously, with leaders, at the least opportunity, trying to change the rules to cling to power for as long as possible. As the African people have come to generally embrace democracy and try to engage political elites, a clearly defined democratic institution is imperative. This will provide citizens with clear choices to make based on the belief that the outcome of the process will truly follow their choices. The rejection of election results and postelection violence clearly demonstrate the lack of trust in the institutions guarding the democratic process.

Again, the interaction between the elites and the governed in Africa's democracies is a very complex one and leaves the people more confused in the process. Some of the confusion includes these questions: Why does democracy speak about freedom of speech and I cannot talk about political issues that are of great concern to me without being arrested or disappearing? Why are leaders more powerful than we expect them to be? Are we not the ones who hired them by casting our vote for them? Why do we constantly lose court cases against the elites? Why do political elites get so rich when voted into public office? Is this the place that one can make money; how does that happen? Why is it that political elites do not consider our concerns even when we loudly voice them? Is this what democracy is all about? Are there any other options that could be explored to make our life better?

Many in Africa have found no alternate options to democracy as practiced on the continent, and political elites are usually reluctant to change the status quo. This has led to tension and instability in some African states even though they claim to practice democracy. North's discussion also expatiates on the essence of institutions in reducing uncertainties. Obviously uncertainties create confusion, and in Africa's democratization process, a critical goal for institution building is to target potential or real uncertainties.

Arguing along the lines of North's view regarding institutions, Hodgson (2006) notes that constraints brought about by institutions allow for choices that may not be found in a situation that does not have such a framework.[3] For instance laws could be written to increase personal safety, and that could be enough justification for the existence of such constraints. Thus institutional constraints benefit, more than they harm, society.

Barry Weingast's analysis (1989) of the U.S. Congress explores the existence of constraints that allow legislators to bargain effectively, since without congressional rules, negotiation and bargaining would be ineffective in determining outcome. Institutional arrangements that provide for judicious use of time through planning enable congressmen and women to estimate the range of achievable outcomes, which in turn enables them to negotiate other bills to bring them within their preferred outcome.

Witold Henisz's (2004) discussion on how political institutions shape the preference of actors, the fractionalization of the legislature, and the level of checks and balances is also worth mentioning. Henisz notes that when the same political party enjoys a majority in two or more levels of government, decision making will be much easier. On the other hand, should there be fractionalization in the legislature with no majority, decision making becomes challenging and may work against the expectations regarding legislators' preferences. However, the available rules should be able to guide legislators in a "what if" situation. As noted by Henisz, an institutional framework that ensures a system of checks and balances structures the balance of authority so that actors may not work to pursue their interests at the expense of others.

In his analysis of veto players, George Tsebelis (2002) notes that actors with the power to veto may work to create instability. Such an institutional framework could work to adversely affect the behavior of people bound by those institutions. Tsebelis also argues that the existence of bureaucracies as a political institution impacts relations within the bureaucracy itself. Bureaucrats who rise through the ranks and political appointees who come to head them have strange relations. The political appointee has the power, while bureaucrats have the knowledge of the day-to-day workings of the bureaucracy.

Neale's discussions (1987) notes that a society's entire set of institutions is functionally related to provide rules for all activities in which members of the society engage. Institutions basically imply "you may" and "thou shall not," and those institutions create and limit the choices available to individuals. Institutions within the society govern people's actions and allow individuals to act with a high degree of confidence in their expectations of how other people will react to and interpret their actions.

Adam Przeworski (2009), in discussing domestic political institutions, notes that even the participation in electoral politics is not completely voluntary, and that institutional rules always shape and organize the act of voting. Electoral rules shape the meanings and consequences of one's vote, which invariably impact one's incentive to participate in the election. Citing the increased participation in elections in contemporary times, Przeworski attributes this to the extension of suffrage, rather than the increased turnout of those eligible. He also notes that institutional frameworks that relate voting to electing structure voters' expression. This emphasizes the extrinsic value of electoral rules as an institution. The idea that the act of voting can result in one's electing a preferred candidate cements legitimacy in what is being done. Though it is not always the case that a voter's preferred candidate is elected, electoral rules help with forecasting and the possibility that electoral outcomes may align with a voter's preference.

Extending Przeworski's discussions, Jennifer van Heerde et al. (2006) noted that the cost of voting, in terms of making a trip to the polling booth, has a tremendous effect on electorates. Electoral laws that affect the costs associated with voting also affect voting turnout. Some of this laws that affect voting could be institutional when for example legislators pass laws to make it hard for people to vote on certain days that are convenient to them. That is, if voting is only allowed on weekdays and an electorate could lose income because they went to exercise their franchise, the cost of voting will be very high. In Africa, an increase in voting cost could come in the form of tension or insecurity on election day. Boko Haram, for instance, threatened to harm Nigerian voters in March 2015 should they actually go to the voting booth. The election was so important to Nigerians that they did not heed that warning. However, the terrorist organization carried out its threat leading to some people losing their lives as a result of honoring their civic responsibilities.

Iris Bohnet and Yael Baytelman (2007) argue that institutions serve two purposes: First, institutions constrain individuals from being driven by greed and not pursuing the common good. And second, institutions protect and nurture peoples' intrinsic motivation, which includes their engaging in civic responsibilities and their willingness to trust and be trustworthy.

Stephen Barley and Pamela Tolbert (1997) note the organic nature of institutions. They argue that institutions and actions are linked, and that though institutions can shape behavior, individuals can also modify institutions. Institutions are created, maintained, and changed through people's action. Barley and Tolbert's examination of the nature of institutions also has implications for institutional development in Africa. If institutions are organic, what role could traditional institutions play in Africa's institutional development, especially the institutionalization of democracy? Could there be an African version of the concept and practice of democracy?

NATURE OF INSTITUTIONS AND INSTITUTIONAL DESIGN

One of the conundrums that African countries face is the nature and type of institutional design that is conducive to building strong states. Institutions are critical to Africa's stability and development whether we are talking about the political, economic, social, or security aspects of the respective states. United States President, Barack H. Obama, on his first trip to Africa in 2009 after he had won the 2008 elections, noted that Africa does not need strong men, but rather strong institutions. Building strong states seems to be a paradox in most Africa states. This is because the relationship between nation building[4] and political consolidations seems to be miles apart.

Although nation building requires strong and stable institutional foundations, these institutions seem incompatible with leaders' power consolidation in Africa. Some African leaders spend a significant part of their tenure in office trying to hold on to power. Again, some may feel they have not done enough and want to continue to remain in office in order to achieve a decent level of nation building considered a positive "legacy." Leaders who could not achieve any meaningful development find themselves in a dilemma when their tenure in office expires and they are unable to extend their stay due to the existence of some workable rules or institutions. Other states without strong institutions are able to twist the arm of the legislative wing to change the constitution to guarantee them an extension for at least another term to get some nation building business done. Yet other leaders are so powerful that they stay in perpetuity and still are not able to build strong states.

This supposedly "wild goose chase" scenario need not happen, since nation building and power consolidation complement each other very well. However in most African states, the preoccupation with power consolidation has led to fewer policy considerations for nation building and development. As Claude Ake notes, the issue of the economy has not yet been on the agenda since independence. Just like the struggle for independence, power consolidation in post-independent African states is a zero-sum game. Time and again, the priority has been how to consolidate political power.

Regarding institutional design, we would be naïve to think that those who develop laws, norms, rules, are not rational actors. Their self-interest is always a significant part of the nature of the institutions developed. It is also equally important to note that those affected by those institutions are not naïve either. So the questions that need to be sorted out have to do with the extent to which institutions take into consideration that nature of the society and societal needs, and how this relates to elite preferences. This is not to suggest an altruistic institution, but rather that which accommodates societal needs of both institutional drafters and the people.

Institutions, noted Phillip Pettit (1996), have the tendency to create certain kinds of awareness, and designers need to be aware of that. Pettit notes, for example, that if laws are made to curtail certain types of deviant behaviors, though individuals are assumed to behave rationally, those who hitherto would not have considered that behavior immediately make calculations regarding what the cost/benefits are for their specific situation. For instance a law to ban the use of ammunition would actually raise awareness in those who otherwise might not even consider owning arms. The notion that people behave rationally cannot explain why adult children continue to give parents monthly allowances. There may be other motivations for such behaviors than rational choice (Pettit, 1996). This could be sheer love for parents or certain intrinsic life benefits inexplicably understood by the specific individual. In institutional design this could be troubling in that the intended outcome could be mitigated by such behaviors. The complexity of human interaction is critical for institutional design; however that is the basis of the institutional design itself.

Another aspect of institutional design has to do with the overall effect of smaller adjustments to existing institutions. Since people generally are skeptical of change due to unintended consequences, a change to the status quo could also be viewed as benchmarks (Coram, 1996). Progressive or evolutionary changes are the most preferred option. However, as scholars have noted, such smaller changes could have dramatic consequences. The Condorcet voting paradox is a classic example of this situation where designers' preferences may lead to ineffective institutions.[5]

Though new institutions may promise efficiency in ensuring development, existing traditional institutions are critical to the success and sustainability of institutional changes and design. Because every society has its own cultures and beliefs, typically described as its "world view" (Dryzek, 1996, it is appropriate that new institutions take that into consideration. The challenge and dilemma for African societies is how much premium they would like to put on existing traditional societies and cultures in the effort to develop new and effective institutions.

Post-independence Africa has not shown much interest in incorporating preexisting, societal worldviews into institution building. One critical issue has to do with the worldview of colonialism, and the extent to which African elites did not dismantle colonial structures after independence. Some of these structures are language and the continued impact on Africa's language policies, justice systems, and relationship between the government and the governed. There is a general belief within Western political culture that the separation of church and state is the best way to go to avoid religious influences on state structures and government. However, religion plays a very significant role in African traditional culture, structures, and day-to-day life, as noted by scholars such as John S. Mbiti. Other issues to consider are the role of the chieftaincy institution in

contemporary African political systems. What is the role of tradition conflict resolution systems in contemporary Africa's justice systems? Sierra
Leone has incorporated the chieftaincy system into its governing structure by allocating twelve parliamentary seats to chiefs. Rwanda has incorporated traditional conflict resolution systems into its justice systems.
Botswana is also on record to have incorporated aspects of its traditional
systems into the governing structures.

The imperative of incorporating traditional systems in state structures
goes to the core of the issue of the legitimacy of contemporary institutions and to injecting transitivity[6] into institutional design and building.
There is no doubt that the people need to have a "congruent spirit" with
the existing or new institutions as noted by Claus Offe (1996). This is an
important aspect of institution building. The compatibility of new institutions to existing institutions reduces hostility toward new institutions
and increases the prospect that the new institution will survive.

Morality—a particular system of values and principles of conduct
held by a particular people or society—is a critical element of institutional design that goes to the very basis of institutional legitimacy. The extent
to which an institution fits into the moral fiber of an individual explains
the sustainability of that institution. Creating working institutions in Africa has been a challenge, and this could be explained by evaluating the
premium that elites put on those institutions. In other words, what are
the values of those institutions?

In his discussion of "Institutional Morality," Russell Hardin (1996)
notes that the relationship between institution and individual action is
problematic. This relationship goes beyond rationality and into issues of
identity and values. African elites have constantly ignored creating sustainable institutions, not because those institutions are difficult to establish, but because of how those institutions fit into their [elite] personal
values and those of the society in general. From the elites point of view,
do these institutions enable them to maximize the benefit of their positions both now and when they are out of office? One wonders why there
are still incidences of extremism and violence, internally displaced persons (IDPs) situation, and refugeeism after international donors have
spent millions of dollars to help African governments build effective institutions to forestall instability and conflicts within the respective societies. As part of efforts to reduce global insecurities, how to deal with
insecurities in Africa has been a concern to the international community.

Perhaps we should be looking at incorporating traditional African values into institutional design. The freeness and fairness of elections in Africa have always been questioned—not because the elections were not organized by fair means, but because of how close the election process is to individual values or how electoral outcomes in the past have confirmed those values. It is no surprise that the pre-election and immediate postelection periods generate tensions due to the assessment of the value of the process.

The enduring nature of institutions is also a significant piece of institutional design. To what extent is an institution compatible with the general perception of public beliefs? Immanuel Kant (1795) argues that perception compatibility is an enduring element of institutional design. In explaining "perception" and "institutional endurance," Kant mentions a "publicity principle." Here he notes that only few people in the society happen to be privy to the underlying maxim of institutional design.

In Plato's "pure democracy" world this will not be an issue since the entire citizens of the society will be part of the institutional development process. However, in contemporary, representative, political societies, not all citizens get the opportunity to engage in the discussions pertaining to institutional design. Representatives are assumed to act as either agents or trustees. They are agents when they do exactly what the people have elected them to do in government. In this case, if for instance the constituency asked the representative to achieve a specific outcome in the bargaining and governing process, the representative does just that. When representatives are assumed to be trustees, in making governing decisions on behalf of their constituency, they behave like experts and balance their personal preferences with their constituents' preferences.

As noted earlier, in the decision-making process, we cannot ignore the fact that representatives could make rational decisions in terms of their nondisclosure of certain maxims in arriving at those decisions, and presenting the outcomes to the constituents as the only prudent option. Luban (1996), in following up with Kant's "transcendental formula of public law,"[7] notes that whether or not such information regarding the underlying maxim of institutional design is made public depends on the process of electing representatives. If the selection process is judged to be fair, then such public disclosures are not necessary and withholding such information is appropriate. Ultimately, institutional designers need to know where the general perception of their constituents lies to assure some degree of compatibility and endurance.

Implementation of the institution is another key element of institutional design. New institutions are meant to provide new opportunities for the citizens, and to enhance their well-being. To the extent that these institutions are not counterproductive and allow for smooth interplay of daily discussions and negotiations, institutional design would have achieved its purpose. In Africa, the lack of democratic consolidation could be a challenge.

The balance between power consolidation and nation building has been a great challenge to most of these countries. This has led to the development of fragile states interspersed with ethnic rivalries and marginalization. As a result, institution building and implementation is viewed with skepticism, and elites are not really sure of the future impact of institutions on their personal lives. Thus the situation has led to the reduction of their commitment to institutional development and implementation.

Structures that enforce institutional implementation are for the most part nonexistent. Naming and shaming political elites do not have the intended negative impact to force a change in attitude since ethnic alliances are stronger than the realities of institutional consequences. Kenneth Shepsle (1996) describes how imperfect institutional enforcement could alter feasible outcomes that are expected. This situation, coupled with the fact that the majority of the people have no idea regarding the full extent of institutional interplay, may become frustrating and lead to apathy toward institutions.

The flexibility of institutional design system also impacts the durability and life span of the institution. The United States Constitution is one such document that shows that institutions are not written in stone, and that the "spirit" underlying institutions can be applicable to changing situations. As already noted, institutions shape behavior and the assumption will be that the institution's rigidity should be enforced to ensure predictable behaviors. However, parts of the U.S. Constitution have been subjected to different interpretations implicitly or explicitly contained in the Constitution. On some occasions, the U.S. Supreme Court has overturned or reviewed its initial rulings on Constitutional questions. An example is *Plessy v. Ferguson*[8] (1896), which legally instituted "two Americas" in public places within the United States based on the interpretation by the justices at the time of some of the clauses of the Fourteenth Amendment. The famous 1954 Supreme Court ruling in *Brown v. Board of Education*[9] reversed this interpretation and effectively abolished segregation at public places in the United States.

Allowing flexibility in the design of African institutions is a step in the right direction judging from the fact that society is organic and institutions should be made to respond to the reality of the time. This is not to suggest that there should be wild shifts in behaviors as a result of such flexibilities.

For African states transitioning to democracy, and many others consolidating their democratic systems, the responsibility falls on the legislators and elected officials to be architects of institutional design. The challenge then becomes the perception accorded such institutions regarding their legitimacy. It has been taken for granted that Western democratic institutions adopted in African states are by default legitimate. The question then becomes this: If these institutions are legitimate, why are elected officials and elites not committed to the design and implementation of those institutions?

This book tries to address fundamental challenges that states in Africa face in developing viable institutions. It starts with a fundamental belief that we cannot talk about development in Africa unless we have somehow dealt with the issue of institutional challenges. These challenges are not limited to the adoption of foreign institutions, but include ones that have substantial roots in domestic norms that define the nature of African society itself. The institutional challenges in some cases have to do with the incompatibility of foreign and domestic institutions. The fundamental issue is the understanding of African societies, African culture, and other dynamics that have ensured stability in the past, and for which special recognition needs to be accorded as African states incorporate foreign institutions into institution building.

The little attention given to domestic norms and other societal realities accounts for weaker institutions and the lack of development on the African continent. We approach this central thesis with a series of research papers stimulating theory-building in addressing critical issues such as gender insensitivity, ethnicity and constitutions, legitimacy and the state, ideologies, and challenges to civil liberties. Each of the chapters has its own thesis and raises questions that could spawn further research.

Chapter 1, which is the introduction of the book, sets out the frame-work within which readers will understand the theme and the issues discussed in the book. Because most of the chapters hinge on institutions in the African setting, the introduction deals with explanations and anal-ysis of institutions and institutional design within the African political environment. Thus it starts with institutional theories and the role of institutions in ensuring stability and development in the politics, society, and the economy of African states. The introduction concludes by high-lighting the theme and arguments made in the rest of the chapters in the book, and how they speak to each other regarding the challenges of dem-ocratic and developmental institutions in Africa.

Chapter 2 examines whether or not democracy has been established in Africa. It argues that the concept of democracy and its practice was "dead on arrival" in Africa. The discussion focuses on the critical elements that weakened the prospects of democracy being established on the African continent. The chapter examines the historical and colonial experiences that challenge current democratic systems in Africa. The chapter also discusses contemporary efforts to potentially resuscitate the democratic process in Africa.

Chapter 3 examines ideologies in the African political systems. It starts with the theme that political ideologies are a significant part of the democratic process. This is because ideology clearly separates the uniqueness of political entities in Africa. This separation allows political parties and governments to efficiently develop substantive policies that further strengthen institutions. The chapter makes a clear distinction be-tween campaign promises and political ideology. It argues that because ideologies shape voters' choices regarding which political party they would prefer, ideology by default is an institution that could guarantee stability and development within states. Ideology also provides a basis for which citizens would hold parties and elites accountable for their policies and performance. Finally, the chapter examines the state of ideol-ogy in Africa's political environment.

Chapter 4 looks at gender and the democratization process in Africa. It examines how institutions shaped women's role in traditional Africa. It also discusses how contemporary institutions, such as international norms and the rise of democracy, are spearheading a process of moving African women from their traditional roles of managing homes into roles where women participate in public decision making. The discussion also emphasizes the role of women's social movement in charting this direction. Thus, the chapter discusses the traditional role of women in African family and economic arenas, and women's role in conflict resolution and peace negotiations.

Chapter 5 examines the issue of legitimacy in the democratization process in Africa. It argues that a critical essence of institutions is the legitimacy of those institutions. Because legitimacy is so important to the sustainability of institutions, the chapter notes that traditional beliefs, norms, and other practices comprise critical parts of the institutional puzzle in Africa. This chapter contrasts traditional societal governing systems with modern state institutions, and argues for the inclusion of traditional institutional systems in institution building in Africa.

Chapter 6 discusses democracy and the politics of petroleum. It examines the dynamics of natural resources and democratic consolidation. It argues that the discovery of petroleum and other mineral resources before democracy poses a major challenge for the democratization process in Africa.

Chapter 7 discusses the challenges to political and other societal freedoms in Africa. As an illustration, it chronicles Oginda Odinga's political life and the efforts made by him to ensure freedom and civil liberties in Kenya.

Chapter 8 discusses the issue of ethnicity and state constitutions in Africa. It asks whether African states' constitutions should be ethnic proof. In other words, African constitutions should recognize the fact that ethnicity is embedded in the social, cultural, and political fabrics of African societies. As a result, conscious efforts need to be made to account for that reality. The chapter also notes that part of the problem of instability in Africa involves the fact that the political process ignores certain ethnicities. Thus an ethnic-proof constitution is a starting point to address issues of instability in most of these states.

NOTES

1. The word "institutions," as used in this book, refers to customs, laws, practices, and rules.

2. For North's detailed analysis of institution and constraints, see Douglas North, "Institutions," *Journal of Economic Perspective* 5 (1, Winter 1991): pp. 77–112.

3. For more analysis of Hodgson's discussion of institutions, see D. Hodgson, "What Are Institutions?," *Journal of Economic Issues* 40 (1, 2006): pp. 1–21.

4. Nation building encompasses the construction of structures such as education, economic stabilization, and security, and infrastructure, governance, and health systems. See Deutsch and Folt, 1966.

5. In this context, a Condorcet institutional paradox ends up with cyclical institutional outcomes that pit the people against each other, since their preferences could not result in more transitive outcomes. In other words, designers' preferences could lead to ineffective rules that do not make sense.

6. Transitivity in this context refers to the extent to which foreign institutions make meaning or are meaningful to the way of life of those that these foreign institutions impact. Both the theoretical and practical workings of new institutions must unequivocally be compatible with existing traditional values.

7. Kant meant that "all actions relating to the rights of other human beings are wrong if their maxim is incompatible with publicity."

8. *Plessy v. Ferguson* (1896) No. 210; Argued April 18, 1896; Decided May 18, 1896; 163 U.S. 537 16S. Ct. 1138; 41L. Ed. 256; 1896 U.S. LEXIS 3390.

9. *Brown v. Board of Education*, argued on December 9, 1952; re-argued on December 8, 1953, and decided on May 17, 1954; 347 U.S. 483, 74 S. Ct. 686; 98 L Ed 873; 1954 U.S. LEXIS 2094; 53 Ohio Op. 326; 38 A.L R. 2d 1180.

TWO

Democracide

*Who Killed Democracy in Africa? Clues of the Past,
Concerns of the Future*

Ali A. Mazrui

The democratization process and democratic consolidation in Africa are challenging phenomena. Democracy as practiced in Africa has, over the years, needed prodding, cajoling, and sometimes the application of both internal and external threats to get it back on track. Such threatening measures, especially those from within the state, highlight the dynamics of how democracy and democratic transitions should proceed within African societies. This chapter examines critical institutional elements that may have killed (hence the word "democracide," used as in "genocide" or "homicide") and continue to challenge democratic institutions in Africa. The chapter also examines the historical and colonial experiences that challenge contemporary democratic systems, and current efforts at resuscitating the democratic process in Africa.

In Africa, while written constitutions are a feature of the twentieth century, constitutionalism—a process of political rules and obligations that bind both governors and the governed, both kings and ordinary citizens—is a much older phenomenon. There is no constitutionalism under absolute monarchs or absolute presidents. Constitutionalism is of necessity a version of limited government. Many societies in Africa before colonialism did endeavor to limit the powers of their rulers.

In Uganda, for example, precolonial constitutionalism was best realized in Northern Uganda. The Northern societies might have been stateless, but they certainly were not constitutionless. Some groups were
"tribes without rulers"—but they were not "tribes without rules." On the
other hand, monarchies in the South were often absolutist. They had de
facto constitutions that gave all powers to groups such as the Kabaka. But
having a constitution is not the same thing as having constitutionalism.
Where rulers have almost unlimited powers, constitutionalism is stifled.

Written constitutions arrived in Africa as colonialism was coming to
an end. Major dilemmas confronted African countries. Tanganyika (lately
Tanzania) considered whether an army was a good state institution to
have at all. Uganda under Milton Obote discussed whether having monarchies was at all sensible. Later Uganda under Yoweri Museveni debated whether having political parties was not a dangerous idea. Issues of
order, stability, and freedom have always been at stake in these fundamental reappraisals. Such considerations not only open for debate the
appropriate political system that has wider support, but also signal the
presence of certain existing, relevant institutions that could hinder the
democratic process.

In analyzing the prospects of democracy in Africa, it may be necessary
to distinguish between "ultimate goals" and "necessary instruments" for
achieving them. It would make sense for Africa to distinguish between
fundamental rights and instrumental rights. The right to vote, for example, is an instrumental right designed to help the achievement of the
fundamental right of government by consent. The right to a free press is
an instrumental right designed to achieve an open society and freedom of
information.[1]

By the same token we can distinguish between "democracy as means"
and "democracy as goals." The most fundamental goals of democracy are
probably four in number. First is to make the rulers accountable and
answerable for their actions and policies. Second, it makes the citizens
effective participants in choosing those rulers and in regulating their actions. Third, it allows for an open society and a transparent economy as
transparent as possible. And last, it makes the social order fundamentally
just and equitable to the greatest number possible. Accountable rulers,
actively participating citizens, open society, and social justice—those are
the four fundamental ends of democracy.[2]

How to achieve these goals has elicited different means. In making the rulers more accountable, some democracies (like the United States) have chosen separation of powers and checks and balances, while other democracies (like the United Kingdom) have chosen the more concentrated notion of sovereignty of Parliament. These are different means toward making the executive branch more accountable and answerable in its use of power.

On the issue of open society, there is also a difference in how the United States and Great Britain regulate freedom of the press and speech. The United States has a highly permissive legal system regarding freedom of speech, but restricts public opinion more. The United Kingdom has a more restrictive legal system regarding freedom of the press, but tolerates public opinion more.[3]

Looking back after the initial burst of patriotism, op-ed columnist and *Slate* editor Michael Kinsley has expressed a similar view in a *Washington Post* article:

> The United States political system protects freedom of speech from formal suppression better than any other nation on earth. But American culture is less tolerant of aberrant views and behavior than many others, and that tolerance has eroded further since Sept. 11. And as conservative culture warriors like to point out—or, indeed, complain (as in the political correctness debate)—a society's norms are set by the culture as much as by the political system. In a country such as Great Britain, the legal protections for free speech are weaker than ours, but the social protections are stronger. They lack a First Amendment, but they have thicker skin and a greater acceptance of eccentricity of all sorts.[4]

If the goals of democracy are the same while the means for achieving them differ, are there African means of achieving those same four goals of accountability of rulers, participation of the citizens, openness of the society, and greater social justice? That is the challenge facing constitution makers in Africa—how to keep the democratic goals constant while looking for democratic means more appropriate to Africa.

TOWARD DEMOCRATIZING DEVELOPMENT

This section describes the positive benefits of democracy as witnessed in the developed world. It includes economic development and other positive conditions that enhance the dignity of the people.

The second big issue about democracy in Africa concerns its relationship to development. Theories of economic development, widely perceived as a Western-centered idea, including Walt W. Rostow's have stipulated the stages necessary for development. Many have discounted these stages as merely the history and development of the Western world. However, if Africa wants to cling to the practice of democracy, which is largely a Western political philosophy, then serious considerations should be accorded these stages of development. On the relationship between democracy and development in Africa, one crucial question has persisted: Which is cause and which is effect: Is Africa underdeveloped because it is primarily undemocratic, or is Africa undemocratic because it is primarily underdeveloped?

There is a third dimension—stability—a social-political precondition for both sustainable development and durable democracy. This third dimension is often treated either as part of the package of development or as part of the package of democracy, when in fact it should be treated as a kind of independent variable.

Africa's three greatest needs are development, democracy, and stability—but not necessarily in that order. Alleviation of poverty is one of the fruits of democratized development. Alleviation of poverty is one of the gains when democracy and development are jointly stabilized and truly humanized.

How has Africa been faring in these areas of development, democratization, stabilization, and the fruit of alleviation of poverty? First let us explore what these words mean. What does "development" mean, for example? Economists naturally focus on issues like resource flows, levels of economic diversification, domestic mobilization of savings and investment, national productivity, and per capita income.[5]

And yet high levels of performance in those areas are achieved only after other measurements of development have already taken place. The most crucial may be partly cultural, having to do with the proper fusion of existing cultures with competing external ones, rather than purely economic. Development in promoting performance and mobilization of domestic savings and investment capital may need to be preceded by development in the following areas: enhancement of managerial skills, transformation of gender relations between men and women as producers, and a redefinition of the work ethic as a discipline of the education system.

Colonialism damaged the work ethic among African males much more than among African females.[6] Laws and rules about corruption need to be redefined to make them more culturally viable. For example, certain forms of ethnic nepotism should be treated with greater understanding than certain forms of bribery. Lighter penalties for nepotism and tougher penalties for bribery may be needed. Ethnic favoritism should be regulated rather than outlawed;[7] and Africa's schools and universities should be reformed to make them more skill relevant and more culturally relevant.[8]

The primary economic problem in Africa has never been structural adjustment. The problem has always been how to carry out cultural readjustment. The readjustment would not be a demotion of African culture.

The readjustment that is needed in culture is a better balance between the continuities of African culture and Africa's borrowing from Western culture. Until now Africa has borrowed Western tastes without Western skills, Western consumption patterns without Western production techniques, urbanization without industrialization, secularization (erosion of religion) without scientification. Would Africa have been better off if it had retained its own tastes while borrowing Western skills—instead of absorbing Western tastes and retaining its own lower levels of skills? Would Africa have been better off with African consumption patterns and Western production techniques instead of the reverse?

The Japanese after the Meiji Restoration in 1868 asked themselves: "Can we economically modernize without culturally Westernizing?" The Japanese said, "YES—we shall seek Western techniques and maintain the Japanese spirit." They retained Japanese tastes; and expanded their Western skills. Following World War II, Japan economically interlocked specifically with the American economy—even displacing American dominance in areas like the automobile industry—without giving up their Japanese spirit.[9]

The Turks abolished the fez,[10] replaced the Arabic alphabet, discouraged the hijab, and attempted to become European (Deringil, 1993, p. 9). They have tried to combine Western tastes with Western skills.

Unlike both the Japanese and the Turks, postcolonial Africans decided to culturally Westernize without economically modernizing. The African strategy has been the worst of both worlds. Africa therefore needs a fundamental cultural, rather than a structural, adjustment to create a new equilibrium between tastes, values, and skills.

Let us now return to the fate of democracy in Africa. Who killed democracy in Africa? This has been the supreme political "who done it" of the first fifty years of Africa's postcolonial era.

DEMOCRACIDE: THE MURDER OF DEMOCRACY IN AFRICA

Democracy as conceptualized in Western political history has its foundation on the sociocultural and political struggles of the respective Western societies. If a fundamental element of democracy is stability, then culture and other belief systems are critical to democracy's survival. The question of whether or not democracy has actually taken foot in Africa could be analyzed when we examine a string of suspects that have emerged from Africa's political history. For the purpose of simplification, let me personify the forces at work.

The magician who came in from the North: This suspect symbolizes the first phase of democratization when magic models of governance were brought into Africa from the temperate zone of the Northern hemisphere. In former British Africa, this meant the adoption in Ghana, Nigeria, Uganda, Kenya, and elsewhere the Westminster magic model of parliamentary government.[11]

The magic that came in from the North was the fascination, the spell cast by Western ways. Africans were mesmerized into uncritical importation of an alien paradigm. This was the phase of high political imitativeness as Africans imitated Western forms, but not Western democratic substance. A major disconnect existed between the imported institutions and the cultural realities of Africa.

While former British Africa tried to imitate the Westminster model, French Africa actually voted in 1958 for continuing colonization by France of their territories. The 1958 referendum gave birth to the Fifth Republic of France, which attracted some imitation from the former colonies.

The imported paradigm did not work as expected. The drift started toward either anarchy (too little control) or tyranny (too much government control). States such as Ghana, Tanzania, and Zambia moved toward a tyrannical one-party state, while others such as Congo and Angola were mired in the realities of the international system, such as the Cold War. Several decades of colonialism and its effect on social behaviors and governmental relations needs to be revisited. For example the colonial administration instituted a top-down governing strategy in which the colonized states just take instructions from the colonial power without questioning. However, by questioning the governing structures, democracy as practiced in the contemporary world does just the opposite.

The opportunity to question the governing structures, unfortunately, has threatened democratic governance in Africa. Political leaders have viewed this criticism as a threat to their hold on power and have resorted to repression, extrajudicial killings, and other human rights abuses to silence criticism (Wiafe-Amoako, 2014). Did the magician who came in from the North turn out to be not an instructor of democracy for Africa, but perhaps a suspect in the murder of African democracy?

There were other suspects behind the mystery of who killed African democracy—for example: *the soldier who came in from the barracks.* On the eve of independence African soldiers had been grossly underestimated as a political force. Even after military mutinies had occurred in 1960 in the former Belgian Congo, African elites were slow to recognize the short distance from an army mutiny to an army coup. By 1963 Togo had not only a coup, but also Africa's first presidential assassination—the murder of Sylvanus Olympio. It was the year of the birth of the Organization of African Unity and the charter condemned "political assassination in all its forms."

By January 1966, Nigeria, Africa's giant, had its first coup. A month later Kwame Nkrumah, the icon of Pan-Africanism, was overthrown in Ghana. A string of other coups followed. [12]

The military's role in African politics can also be understood as a consequence of how African political elites have exploited that institution to suppress political opponents under the guise of ensuring domestic stability. But the true intention is to selfishly hold and consolidate political power. If the military has been unconventionally used internally to ensure domestic stability, it comes as no surprise if the military takes over power and rule, since it has come to believe that it is the only institution capable of creating an environment of domestic stability and security. Thus democracy has abdicated its role of ensuring stability and security, and the military has stepped in.

The military's role in government should not be seen as a mere hunger for political power on the part of the military, but rather within a broader context of democracy-security nexus, and the interlocking relationship between traditional beliefs and norms and modern concepts such as democracy.

In apartheid South Africa, massive police and military services were employed to support the unsustainable "democratic [apartheid] rule" that was instituted. In some African states such as Ghana, Nigeria, and Burkina Faso, long periods of military rule have resulted in the transition to fairly sustainable democracies, though some military rulers have run and won elections while others have totally relinquished power. What is not clear is why the military finally decided to transition to civilian rule.

The spy who came in from the cold is also a suspect in the death of democracy in Africa. This was the period when Western powers and Western business permitted their African favorites to be corrupt and repressive for as long as they were anticommunist. Taking the correct side in the Cold War between the Atlantic Alliance and the Warsaw Pact became the litmus test of legitimacy.[13] Mobutu Sese Seko, and other dictators like him, lasted from the 1960s to the 1990s with the West even defending him against internal civil disobedience.

The Soviet side also played its part in the ideological spying and subversion that helped to kill democracy in countries that range from Ethiopia to Mozambique, from Somalia to Angola. There were echoes from John le Carré's *The Spy Who Came in from the Cold* novel.[14]

Another suspect responsible for killing African democracy is *the cultural half-caste who came in from Western schools and did not adequately respect African ancestors*. Institutions were inaugurated without reference to cultural compatibilities, and new processes were introduced without respect for continuities. Ancestral standards of property, propriety, and legitimacy were ignored.

When writing a new constitution for African nations, these elites asked themselves, "How does the House of Representatives in the United States structure its agenda? How do the Swiss cantons handle their referenda? I wonder how the Canadian federation would handle such an issue."[15] On the other hand, these African elites almost never asked, "How did the Banyoro, the Wolof, the Igbo, or the Kikuyu govern themselves before colonization?" In the words of the Western philosopher, Edmund Burke, "People will not look forward to posterity who never look backward to their ancestors" (Burke, 2001, p. 184).

The final suspect who killed African democracy is perhaps *the angry spirits of the ancestors themselves.* Have the ancestors cursed the first two or three generations of postcolonial Africans because of an apparent contempt for the legacy of the ancestors? Many Africans are ashamed of indigenous religions as a result of vicious penetration of foreign religions such as Christianity and Islam. For example, indigenous religions have no public space in the curriculum of schools; there is no celebration of special indigenous sacred days for traditional religions. Africa celebrates festivals like Christmas and Eid el-Fitr every year—but almost no African country has set aside a special holiday to celebrate traditional indigenous religions.

Have the ancestors responded with an all-powerful curse upon Africa's generations? "Your roads will decay, your railways will rust, your factories will grind to a standstill, your schools will stink with overcrowding and crumble with incompetence, your soil will fight so-called desertification and your economies suffocate under your new globalization. Your democracy will smolder like a dying bush fire, after a drizzle of hate." [16]

In this murder story, who is truly guilty of assassinating African democracy? As in the case of Agatha Christie's famous novel *Murder on the Orient Express*, there was not just one murderer. Every suspect on the Orient Express had a hand in the murder after all. Similarly, all the suspects in Africa's democracide did indeed contribute to the death of democracy. The magician who came in from the North signifies a false foreign start in democratization; the soldier who came in from the barracks is a symbol of power from the means of destruction; the subversive spy who came in from the cold portrays Africa's ideological perversion under Cold War conditions; the cultural half-caste from Western schools includes Africa's Westernized elites who totally ignore cultural realities of Africa; and the angry spirits of the ancestors convey the widely held beliefs within African societies of curses the ancestors can unleash should one violate any of the indigenous traditions.

But democracy can have a kiss of life—a kind of kiss from a Prince Charming who brings it back to life. Democracy needs miracle workers of resuscitation. Indeed, is African democracy really dead? Signs of life are already in evidence. Is African democracy capable of first-aid resuscitation? If so, who is the miracle worker who is to do it? Who is Prince Charming with the kiss of life?

TOWARD RESUSCITATING THE DEMOCRATIC ORDER

Who was the Prince Charming who has been trying to resuscitate African democracy? Who are the miracle workers?

In the first place, Africa's prodemocracy movements from the 1980s that have demanded of African dictators greater accountability and insisted on better governance need to be recognized.[17] Liberation struggle groups such as in Angola (1975), Mozambique (1980), Namibia (1992), and South Africa (1994) are still in power and some of them may not pass the test of being democratic. Likewise groups that rose up and deposed African dictators in states like Uganda, Ethiopia, and Eritrea in the 1990s cannot be described as being democratic according to Freedom House rankings. However, prodemocracy movements and activities in states such as Zambia and Malawi, and the reforms in the political space, are steps in the right direction.

Certain Westernized African cultural half-castes who have "seen the light" could also be seen as key elements in the effort to resuscitate African democracy. These include Léopold Senghor who retired voluntarily in 1980; Mwalimu Julius K. Nyerere, in 1985; Nelson Mandela, in 1998; and Daniel Arap Moi, in 2003. Others include founding fathers who permitted themselves to be defeated at the polls, such as Zambia's Kenneth Kaunda; Malawi's Hastings Banda; and KANU, the former ruling party of Kenya. Mention can also be made of second generation leaders who let themselves be defeated at the polls. These include Senegal's Abdou Diouf, out after twenty years in power for himself and forty years in power for his political party; and Kenya's Daniel Arap Moi after a quarter of a century in power.

Soldiers formerly from the barracks who have "seen the light" could also be credited in the effort at resuscitating democracy in Africa. This includes Olusegun Obasanjo of Nigeria who was a military ruler from 1976 to 1979, and was later elected president in 1999. In Ghana, Jerry John Rawlings transformed from brutal dictator to new democrat after two military coups initially brought him to power, and then became president after two electoral successes confirmed his reformed status under the Constitution of the Fourth Republic of Ghana.

Mention can also be made of Western Cold Warriors who have "seen the light" and no longer perpetuate African dictators as part of a struggle against communism. Examples include Mobutu Sese Seko, who could no longer depend on his Western allies to save him in 1996, and President Daniel Arap Moi, who was under pressure in his last years for greater accountability on issues of corruption. The World Bank and the IMF (International Monetary Fund) now concede the economic relevance of good governance when in fact they once resisted political conditionality;[18] smaller European countries more clearly tie their foreign aid to democratic performance in Africa and are more sensitive to human rights; and political apartheid has at last been permitted to collapse without invoking the fear of a communist takeover of South Africa.

Also significant in the discourse of elements resuscitating democracy in Africa are the impact of the collapse of communism in Eastern Europe, the discrediting of the one-party state, and the decline of Leninist radicalism in the politics of the Third World. Marxist-Leninist regimes in Portuguese-speaking Africa have disappeared outright. Ethiopia has been experimenting with a federation of cultures rather than a Leninist junta. Racial and ideological pluralism have replaced apartheid in South Africa as Mozambique is trying out multiparty democracy. Currently Tunisia and Morocco show promising examples in multiparty systems and democratization for the rest of Africa's North.

GENDER: THE MISSING AGENDA

The fault lines of African democracy have included the ethnic fault line, religious fault line, regional fault line, the divide between political generations (old politicians versus new), and the class divide (as affected by structural adjustment, for better or worse). The divide still missing in the grand design has been the gender factor. Throughout Africa inadequate planning for the empowerment of women in the political process pervades.

Postcolonial Africa has started using women in senior diplomatic positions more by default than by design and more readily than in almost any other major public service. Uganda has had a woman foreign minister and a woman vice president sooner than the United States had a woman secretary of state. The United States has still not had a woman vice president. Uganda has also had a number of senior, female ambassadors since independence—at posts that have ranged from Accra to Paris, Copenhagen to Washington, and Paris to Ottawa.

Paris itself has had a diverse number of African women ambassadors representing a range of political regimes from Ghana to Tanzania, from the African National Congress (ANC) to Uganda. The ANC Envoy, Ms. Dulcie September, was indeed assassinated in Paris in 1988, probably by agents of apartheid.

The most famous African woman of the 1970s was Elizabeth Bagaya, Princess of Toro. Dictator Idi Amin made her ambassador and then foreign minister of Uganda. He then tried to humiliate this proud African woman with allegations of sexual misconduct at a French airport. The lies were a disgrace to Idi Amin rather than to the princess.

The most famous African woman of the 1980s was Winnie Mandela. Again this was not through a planned, political design. In a sense Winnie Mandela's ascent to political prominence was in the same tradition as Mrs. Corazon Aquino of the Philippines (in the wake of a martyred husband), Ms. Benazir Bhutto in Pakistan (in the wake of a martyred father), and Mrs. Sirimavo Bandaranaike in Ceylon (now Sri Lanka—in the wake of a martyred husband.) Winnie Mandala—like the other women—was another illustration of female succession to male martyrdom.

Under Black rule South Africa, like Zimbabwe before it, did experiment with a system of disguised racial reservation of seats for whites at least for a while. But should not planned governance in Africa as a whole include a strategy of gender reservation of seats? Uganda under Yoweri Museveni has made an impressive start with women parliamentarians, but a schedule of empowerment is needed.

Where is this kind of gender planning most likely to happen? Apart from places like Uganda, the most likely laboratories of gender planning in Africa may turn out to be Muslim countries. For one thing, Muslim societies are more used to gender separation in other areas of social life. Second, Muslim countries like Pakistan and Egypt have already experimented with special seats for women. Third, Muslim African countries like Somalia and Libya have experimented with gender regiments in the armed forces—in a continent where soldiers remain among the major actors in politics. Fourth, it is a Muslim country—Algeria—that seems to have led the way in using women in the air force, and the air force is often a major influence on political strategies in Africa.

In contemporary times, however, some African states have aggressively pursued higher female representations in the legislature. Electoral laws have assured women representation in Morocco, Botswana, and Tanzania, thereby guaranteeing women participation in the policy formulation process. Uganda for instance had 112 women out of 375 total seats in the 2011 National Assembly. The women were directly elected from districts allocated to women representations. Morocco also had sixty seats reserved for women in the 2011 elections. This was an increase from thirty in 2002.

THE SEX CODE AND THE CONSTITUTIONAL ORDER

Constitutionalism is not only about relations between families and genders, perennial and vital as these are; nor is constitutionalism only about political participation and ethnic accommodation, crucial as these dimensions are to be considered. Constitutionalism is also about the limits of state power in the lives of private individuals. They say "an Englishman's home is his castle," ready to be defended by him even against all unwarranted officialdom. Under what circumstances is "an African's home his kraal," ready to be defended by him even against state intrusion? Constitutionalism is therefore also about the curbing of state power from intruding too far into the private life of the individual.

John Stuart Mill (1806–1873) drew a distinction between self-regarding actions, which have consequences only for the person doing them, and other-regarding actions, which have consequences for other people. According to Mill's view of liberty, a democratic government does not interfere in the self-regarding actions of an individual, even if the government or the society disapproves of them (Mill, 1859). Thus, if a man and a woman decide to live in sin and never get married, a democratic government and a free society should not interfere, even if they disapprove of the sinful lifestyle.

In high English society in J. S. Mill's era, it was a bigger scandal to be discovered as being a homosexual than to be discovered as being economically corrupt. What was considered sexual deviation was regarded with greater disapproval than economic deviance—although corruption was more "other-regarding" than homosexuality. What has happened in the West since John Stuart Mill and the imprisonment of Oscar Wilde is a reversal of priorities. There are more and more laws against individual economic deviance (such as kickbacks and bribery) and fewer and fewer regulations to moderate individual sexual practices.

In most of Africa, except the Republic of South Africa, is the order of priority closer to the days of Oscar Wilde in Britain than to the days of "don't ask, don't tell" in the United States? Apart from South Africa (where homosexuality is legalized), are most African governments more targeted against sexual deviance difference than against economic deviance? The governments of Robert Mugabe in Zimbabwe, ex-President Daniel Arap Moi of Kenya, and Yoweri Museveni in Uganda have shown greater indignation against homosexuality than against economic corruption, relatively speaking—though in reality the three governments have often been concerned about both tendencies.

President Museveni played host to President Bill Clinton of the United States in 1998. President Clinton had a sex scandal in 1998; did he use war to divert attention from it? President Museveni had a war scandal in 1999; did Museveni use sex to divert attention from it? Clinton's war-games in 1998 ranged from bombing Afghanistan and Sudan to new confrontations with Iraq; his sex scandal was of course primarily the Monica Lewinsky affair. President Museveni's war scandal in 1999 was the degree of his army's involvement in the conflict of the Democratic Republic of the Congo. His sex diversion in 1999 was the intemperate attack on the gay community in Uganda, and his giving the green light to the police to engage in massive harassment of homosexuals.

In the United States the self-regarding actions of the most powerful man in the country were exploited by his political enemies in 1998. But American public opinion insisted that private adultery was self-regarding and irrelevant for Clinton's public office. The Senate of the United States refused to convict Clinton of "high crimes and misdemeanors."

In Uganda the most powerful man in the land was not cast in the role of the accused but in the role of the accuser. And the real accused were a vulnerable sexual minority (homosexuals) who, even in the West, continue to be exposed to intolerance and violent bigotry. In Zimbabwe, Uganda and Kenya the state seems to be eager to join the heterosexual extremists in their bigotry. In Museveni's Uganda and Mugabe's Zimbabwe homosexual sinners may be victimized by the state—while corrupt officials, politicians, and soldiers often get away with most of their loot. In most of Africa, other-regarding corruption often enjoys more de facto license than self-regarding sexual deviation.

In contrast, some positive reactions are happening in the Western world these days. In much of the Western world the state has been trying to protect homosexuals from the bigotry of heterosexual extremists. The West has learned that individual's private life such as sexual orientations should be left to the efforts of religious and moral institutions.

Constitutionalism in the broader society is supposed to be one of the anchors of stability—helping to define the rules of the game, helping to check excesses of power, seeking to extend democratic rights and due process even to those who might stray to economic deviance, even to those who might manifest sexual difference.

COUNTERTERRORISM VERSUS DEMOCRACY

Democracy was killed in Africa by multiple assassins. And the multiple miracle workers had been in the process of resuscitating democracy. Prospects looked promising—until September 11, 2001.

The aftermath of the attacks on the World Trade Center and the Pentagon has affected not only the issue of war and peace in Afghanistan, but also civil liberties in the United States. In addition, the aftermath has interrupted the democratic revival in Africa. Is this yet another suspect of democracide—the murder of democracy?

Within the United States it has been demonstrated that even a democracy that is more than two hundred years old can be very fragile. One day of terrorist attacks in the United States has demonstrated the following threats to civil liberties in the United States:

1. Hundreds of people are held in detention in the United States without trial.[19]
2. Most of them are detained without their names being made public.
3. The Bush administration considered secret military trials for people suspected of terrorism.[20] Even the Nazi leaders after World War II had public trials in Nuremberg with access to their own lawyers. Some of the Nazi leaders had killed millions of people, not just two or four thousand.
4. Attorney General John Ashcroft wanted people to betray their friends in the hope of getting a U.S. green card or U.S. citizenship. In the McCarthy era in America members of families reported on

each other's alleged communist connections. Now alleged terrorist connections are being sought.

With regard to the impact of September 11, 2001, on the resuscitation of democracy in Africa, the result so far has been antidemocratic. The Federal Bureau of Investigation has been busy in Kenya and Tanzania with a variety of Muslim names. In Tanzania they arrived with sixty names.

In Kenya the government is sometimes way ahead of what the FBI wants it to do in the fight against terrorism. There have been attempts to try to extradite Kenyan citizens to the United States. Not to be outdone in the anthrax debate, Kenya in October 2001 claimed to be the second country after the United States to be targeted with anthrax by unknown terrorists. Not even the U.S. Embassy in Nairobi was impressed by Kenya's claims. Kenya is also on record for drafting an antiterrorism law in 2015 with provisions for curbing media freedom and capping the number of refugees in the country at 150,000. A fierce resistance by the opposition led to the Kenyan Supreme Court's throwing out some of the provisions, including those regarding media freedom. However, other provisions, such as holding suspects for more than twenty-four hours, still remain part of the new bill.

A number of African governments, under pressure from the politics of the war against terrorism, have been getting ready to enact new legislation ostensibly against terrorist threats. The legislation is more likely to be used against either ethnic minorities or political opponents to a regime in Africa. In Uganda there is evidence to suggest that the minister of internal affairs will be given additional powers to harass organizations ostensibly because of their suspected terrorist leanings. Uganda is a country that is already suspicious of ordinary political parties as potentially divisive and has been trying to move toward a "no-party democracy."[21] Uganda also faces ethnic conflicts in the North—conflicts that should be solved by a political process rather than by the heavy hand of antiterrorist measures.

South Africa, which has one of the most liberal constitutions in the world, is under pressure to reduce civil liberties and return to some of the old antiterrorist tactics of the apartheid years. And Robert Mugabe in Zimbabwe is already learning to use the term "terrorist" as a term of political denunciation. In November 2001, President Mugabe threatened to take action against journalists and reporters, describing them as "agents of terrorism."[22]

At the height of the Cold War, democracy in Africa suffered because African governments were allowed to sacrifice civil liberties in the name of fighting communism. Will democracy now suffer because African governments are encouraged to sacrifice civil liberties in the name of combating terrorism?

On the Orient Express of history, African democracy had once been murdered by multiple assassins. And then at a first-aid railway station, multiple miracle workers and Prince Charming started resuscitating African democracy.

In conclusion, by 2001, there were more legal political parties in Africa than ever before, far fewer military regimes than in the 1980s, greater freedom of the press, and more open debate about corruption and mismanagement than was conceivable fifteen years earlier. Some of the new constitutions—like Ethiopia's regionalist idea of a federation of cultures[23]—even respected ethnic ancestors in a new way. African democracy was slowly getting resuscitated.

And then came September 11, 2001. Thousands of people died at the World Trade Center and thousands of Afghans and Iraqis have since been killed. September 11 has had many horrendous casualties. African democracy is in intensive care. Must it also die because of September 11? The African patient was beginning to breathe again. Must the plug be pulled? Who is the new villain behind Africa's democracide?

Let us hope the worst will be averted, resuscitation will be resumed, and a new equilibrium will be found between democracy as means and democracy as ultimate goals in Africa's political experience.

NOTES

1. A discussion on fundamental rights may be found in Milton R. Konvitz, *Fundamental Rights: History of a Constitutional Doctrine* (New Brunswick, NJ: Transaction Publishers/Rutgers University, 2001).

2. For a historical overview of democracy, consult Roland N. Stromberg, *Democracy: A Short, Analytical History* (Armonk, NY: M. E. Sharpe, 1996); and for a contemporary view, see Anthony H. Birch, *The Concepts and Theories of Modern Democracy*, 2nd ed. (London and New York: Routledge, 2001). Specific treatments of African democracy can be found in Obioma M. Iheduru, ed., *Contending Issues in African Development: Advances, Challenges, and the Future* (Westport, CT: Greenwood Press, 2001); and Teodros Kiros, with a preface by K. Anthony Appiah, *Explorations in African Political*

Thought: Identity, Community, Ethics (New York: Routledge, 2001); and for a cultural approach, see Daniel T. Osabu-Kle, *Compatible Cultural Democracy: The Key to Development in Africa* (Peterborough, ON; Orchard Park, NY: Broadview Press, 2000).

3. For discussions on the American and British scene, see Thomas R. Hensley, ed., *The Boundaries of Freedom of Expression & Order in American Democracy* (Kent, OH: Kent State University Press, 2001), and Part IV of David Feldman, *Civil Liberties and Human Rights in England and Wales* (Oxford, UK: Clarendon Press; New York: Oxford University Press, 1993).

4. Michael Kinsley, "Listening to Our Inner Ashcrofts," *Washington Post*, January 4, 2002, p. 27.

5. For discussions, see Dilip Mookherjee and Debraj Ray, eds., *Readings in the Theory of Economic Development* (Malden, MA: Blackwell Publishers, 2001); B. N. Ghosh, *Contemporary Issues in Development Economics* (London and New York: Routledge, 2001); and Yujiro Hayami, *Development Economics: From the Poverty to the Wealth of Nations* (Oxford and New York: Oxford University Press, 2001).

6. For an overview of gender and work in Africa, consult Aderanti Adepoju and Christine Oppong, eds., *Gender, Work and Population in Africa* (London: James Currey and Portsmouth, NH: Heinemann, 1994); and for a specific Kenyan case, see M. Silberschmidt, *Rethinking Men and Gender Relations: An Investigation of Men, Their Changing Roles within the Household, and the Implications for Gender Relations in Kisii District, Kenya* (Copenhagen: Center For Development Research, 1991).

7. This kind of ethnic corruption and favoritism eats away at the basic fairness implicit in a democratic system, and ethnicity becomes an obstacle in Africa's march toward more democratic regimes. Consult, relatedly, E. Ike Udogu, "The Issue of Ethnicity and Democratization in Africa: Toward the Millennium," *Journal of Black Studies* 29 (6, July 1999), pp. 790–808; and Julius O. Ihonvbere, "The 'Irrelevant' State, Ethnicity, and the Quest for Nationhood in Africa," *Ethnic and Racial Studies* 17 (January 1994), pp. 42–60; and for an extended discussion on corruption in Africa, see Kempe Ronald Hope, Sr. and Bornwell C. Chikulo, eds., *Corruption and Development in Africa: Lessons from Country Case-Studies* (New York: St. Martin's Press, 2000).

8. A World Bank paper by a former University of Liberia president lays out the obstacles and some approaches to reforming higher education in Africa; see Mary A. Brown Sherman, *Building Consensus for Higher Education Reform in Africa: Some Reflections* (Washington, DC: World Bank, 1993); and for a regional discussion, see Dickson A. Mungazi and L. K. Walker, *Educational Reform and the Transformation of Southern Africa* (Westport, CT: Praeger, 1997).

9. The two periods of Japanese transformation are described in Ann Waswo, *Modern Japanese Society* (Oxford: Oxford University Press, 1996).

10. Mustafa Kemal Atatürk banned the fez in Turkey in 1925 as part of his modernizing cultural reforms to secularize Turkey.

11. The African experience with democracy is surveyed through various case studies in Larry Diamond, Juan Linz, and Seymour Martin Lipset, eds., *Democracy in Developing Countries*, Vol. 2 (Boulder, CO: Lynne Rienner Publishers, 1988).

12. An overview of the way in which military power took over civilian governments is provided in Ruth First, *The Barrel of a Gun: Political Power in Africa and the Coup* (London: Allen Lane, 1970).

13. For overviews of the African situation in the Cold War, see Fred Marte, *Political Cycles in International Relations: The Cold War and Africa, 1945–1990* (Amsterdam: VU

University Press, 1994); and Zaki Laïdi, *The Superpowers and Africa: The Constraints of a Rivalry, 1960–1990* (Chicago: University of Chicago Press, 1990).

14. This classic novel of the Cold War was first published in the sixties; see John Le Carré, *The Spy Who Came in from the Cold* (New York: Coward-McCann, 1964).

15. This time might be a ripe opportunity to launch discourses on new constitutions; see John Mbaku, "Effective Constitutional Discourse as an Important First Step to Democratization in Africa," *Journal of Asian and African Studies* 31 (June 1996), pp. 39–51.

16. Professor Ali A. Mazrui has used this quote in several of his speaking appointments.

17. See V. Rich, "Africa's 'New Wind of Change,'" *World Today* 48 (7, July 1992), pp. 116–19; and also Julius O. Ihonvbere, "On the Threshold of Another False Start? A Critical Evaluation of Prodemocracy Movements in Africa," in *Democracy and Democratization in Africa: Toward the 21st Century*, ed. E. Ike Udogu (Leiden and New York: E. J. Brill, 1997), pp. 125–42.

18. In fact, M. Ould-Mey, in an article entitled "Democratization in Africa: The Political Face of SAPS," *Journal of Third World Studies* 12 (2, Fall 1996), pp. 122–58, argues that Western donor/lender influence was more important than prodemocracy movements in affecting the positive trend towards democratization.

19. *New York Times*, November 29, 2001, p. 1.

20. See the concerns raised by critics in a report in the *New York Times*, December 29, 2001, p. B7.

21. Consult, for instance, Nelson Kuofir, "No-Party Democracy in Uganda." *Journal of Democracy* 9 (2, April 1998), pp. 49–63.

22. See the Associated Press report, cited in, for instance, *The Hamilton Spectator*, November 24, 2001, p. D2.

23. For more details on the Ethiopian federalism experiment, see Kjetil Tronvoll, *Ethiopia: A New Start?* (London: Minority Rights Group, 2000).

THREE

Political Ideologies and Democratic Consolidation in Africa

Francis Wiafe-Amoako

Ideology—a system of ideas and ideals—usually shapes the basis of economic, social, or political trajectory. With regard to democratic consolidation in Africa, political ideology has the potential to separate the numerous political parties vying for the opportunity to be given the mandate to govern. Thus, it helps structure the parties and clearly differentiates the parties to enable voters to make their choice of which party ultimately becomes the ruling government. Since ideology shapes behavior and the choices people and entities have to make, this chapter argues that ideology by default is an institution.

Africa has had its share of leaders claiming to be leaning toward one ideological strand as opposed to the other. The immediate postindependence era saw a proliferation of ideologies from nationalism to socialism, and even to ones that have leaders' names associated with them—for example, Nkrumahism. Though there may not be a coherent systematic belief that ideology would be useful to a particular political party especially where that party wanted to broaden its base to achieve a majority of the vote, it is clear that party programs are simply not a collection of random ideas, but a carefully planned program of ideas that is consistent with the core beliefs of the party.

In contemporary times, African political parties, consciously or unconsciously, have shunned implicitly or explicitly associating themselves with ideological beliefs and have settled for fluid political manifestos. Such a strategy may well provide the nuances favorable to portray political parties as broad based or inclusive. This includes a laundry list of program promises most of which may not be fulfilled during the tenure of the governing party. This attitude—"I'm for everything and not against anything"—creates a situation that does not differentiate political parties.

The consequences are dire—the most serious being that governing parties may not be held accountable for the promises they make because all the parties seem the same due to similar platforms. It is difficult to judge which party to prefer if the policy outcomes are similar and the parties do not provide the fundamental strategic means of achieving those goals (which could separate the parties). As a result of the inability to differentiate between the parties, ethnicity becomes a filter through which the electorate chooses a candidate.

Political ideology is currently nonexistent or at least not touted in contemporary political discourse in Africa. Parties would prefer to provide a list of programs that they would implement when elected. Parties' manifestos are a mere focus on the current needs of the people. Long-term planning that requires viable institutions as a foundation becomes less of a priority, and this does not enhance democratic consolidation.

The essence of ideology in Africa's political space is reflected in Robert D. Putnam's (1973) definition of ideology as life-guiding systems of beliefs, values and goals, affecting political style and action. Putnam's definition clearly shows the importance of ideology, including helping to shape people's worldview. The seemingly nonexistence of ideology in African political discourse raises the question of the role of political parties in democratic transitions and consolidation.

European political parties have distinguished themselves from each other through their ideological leanings. However, this does not mean that they would only welcome those who support their ideological beliefs. They offer alternatives for how to get to political outcomes through different routes. These different routes are good for democratic consolidation since they not only set parties apart, but also enhance parties' commitments to their stated alternative. It also allows the electorate to seriously consider the alternative routes.

Identifying needs is easy to do. However, the ideological means to address those needs is a huge responsibility for parties vying for the mandate to govern. For example, how does a liberal party view LGBTQ issues as opposed to a conservative party? Is it the case that the conservative party does not want anything to do with LGBTQ issues? The answer is obviously no. Their perspective on how to deal with the issue would enable the electorate to make an informed decision regarding which party to vote for.

Many political parties in Africa are basically similar in terms of their purporting to offer the same policy outcomes. This situation is a perfect breeding ground for ethnic groups to tag on to certain parties no matter the party's view on issues. The attitude will be that if the parties are the same regarding policy goals, then one is more "secure" with a political party whose leadership is from one's ethnic group.

The importance of ideology within African political space cannot be overemphasized especially in the postindependence African states where the hunt for better strategies to move toward stability and development is a priority, and most importantly where development is associated with issues of culture and identity (Falola, 2003). Ideological underpinnings of policies enhance the prospect of building viable institutions to achieve those policies goals.

In China, communist institutions are strong and viable. When the Chinese government decided to open up its economy and to engage the global market, institutions were put in place to support this long-term plan. European political parties seek the same outcome—that is, to develop the economy and enhance the welfare of the people. However the means of achieving those outcomes has differed and the party whose ideological leaning provides the better alternative for societal advancement has won elections.

The situation in the United States provides an even clearer understanding of the dynamics of political ideology. The growing number of Independent members of the electorate—those not identifying as either Democrats or Republicans—has been viewed as an opportunity for the rise of a third party. However, a third party has not been able to absorb the growing number of electoral Independents. In the absence of a third political party, Democrats and Republicans have courted Independents come election time. Independent electorates have not sat on the fence either, but have gone to the polls to either support Republican or Democratic candidates who, though policy goals may be the same, have provided a better means to achieve those goals. Even within the Republican

Party, the rise of the Tea Party (far right-leaning candidates) has forced Republicans to clarify their ideological stance in order to stem the Tea Party insurgency of taking control of the American right.

CONCEPTUAL ANALYSIS OF IDEOLOGY

Ideology carries with it expectations and sometimes nostalgia. The Communist ideology that emerged after the Russian Bolsheviks' Revolution ushered in a societal change. After the collapse of the Soviet Union, when faced with the reality capitalism and individualism, ex-Soviet republics such as Uzbekistan became nostalgic for the old system. Ideologies are "thought systems that serve to defend a particular social order, and broadly express the interests of its dominant or ruling group"[1] (Bamikole, 2012; Mannheim, 1960).

Mannheim's definition of "ideology" separates it from "utopia," which literally describes an attempt to create a highly desirable and close-to-perfect situation. Many contemporary African political and governing parties have platforms that could be described as utopian by nature, and thus governing parties have not been able to achieve the goals that they set during their tenure in office. Karl Popper (1991) noted that Utopia is a very dangerous phenomenon due to the fact that it breeds violence. It is therefore not a surprise to see how dangerous some "democracies" in Africa have become due to the fact that parties and governments lack ideological foundations, and this has created an environment where leaders live under the illusion that they are doing all-of-the-above things and therefore are entitled to hold on to power. The other side of political violence could be seen from the opposition, which does not understand why a single party should be in power for a long time when both political platforms are the same.

Despite the imperative of ideology for Africa's political governing, there are others who argue that the relevance of ideology has waned and that what truly matters is the extent to which a governing party can deliver on growth and development (Bell 1960). This growth and development has not happened yet in most of these African states, and political elites are still preoccupied with holding on to power.

However, ideology has become an important tool with which to discuss governing parties over the years. Frantz Fanon noted "for my part, the deeper I enter into the cultures and the political circles, the surer I am that the great danger that threatens Africa is the absence of ideology" (Fanon, 1988, p. 186).

An analysis of European political parties and their respective ideologies demonstrates how important ideological differences are to democratic consolidation. In Europe, there is a left-right continuum that includes from the left: Communists, Social Democrats/Socialists, New Left parties, and Greens; center: Liberals; right: Christian Democratic parties, Conservatives, and Nationalist parties. Parties to the left, for instance Communist parties, emerged in the twentieth century with an average mean support in the 1950s of about 7.9 percent. In the 1990s the mean support had shrunk to about 3.5 percent.

Obviously the collapse of the Soviet Union and end of the Cold War, both of which put these parties on the defensive, could explain the reason for the decline in the support for European Communist parties or their other strand, "Eurocommunism." Still on the left, the Social Democrats have been very successful and strong in the 1950s through to the 2000s in European states such as Scandinavia, Austria, Germany, the United Kingdom (Labour party), France, and Italy. However the average mean support had dropped from 33.6 percent in the 1950s to 29.9 percent in the 1990s. This decline has not discouraged the Social Democrats to abandon their fundamental ideals in nation building. Green parties have also been gaining grounds in certain European states including Belgium, France, Luxembourg, Finland, Austria, Netherlands, Germany, and Switzerland. Their share of the polity has increased from 2 percent in the 1980s to 4.1 percent in the 1990s and 7.5 percent in the 2000s.

Liberal political ideology has also been significant in European political experience with their average support over 10 percent in the 1990s and currently hovering around 9 percent. Political parties such as Netherland's D66, the United Kingdom's Liberal Democrats, Germany's Free Democrats, and France's Union of French Democracy, have been very instrumental in coalition building.

In the immediate center-right are the Christian Democrats who can be seen in Germany, Luxemburg, Belgium, Ireland, Netherlands, and Austria. The Christian Democrats who are strong advocates of the welfare state in Europe as well as European integration had had a support base of about 20.7 percent in the 1950s but dropped in the 1990s to 14.5 percent.

Conservative parties in Europe have championed fiscal austerity, government efficiency, and stronger emphasis on the private sector as the engine of growth. Though the Conservatives occasionally do not shy away from the government's role in the economy, it has generally not been their priority. Conservatives mean support base has been fairly stable, hovering around 18 percent in the postwar.

The shift in support base for parties has resulted in European political parties having to form coalition governments. This coalition formation has not resulted in the co-optation of smaller political parties. In fact, coalitions have strengthened the ideological stance of smaller parties, resulting in strengthened democracy. This is not the case in Africa where, for lack of ideology, smaller parties are easily co-opted into bigger ones, with examples in countries such as Ghana, Nigeria, and Kenya.

In the United States the two parties (Republican and Democratic) have constantly sought to distinguish between themselves. The realignment of the Democratic Party's base in the South to the Northeast and Western United States in the 1930s has been well documented. The shift in African American votes from Republican to Democrat around this time period has also been documented. The power struggle in the U.S. government branches (executive and legislative) has demonstrated the role of ideology in shaping and implementing party goals. As discussed earlier, this has also given voters the opportunity to reject the parties from time to time when the policy consequence from the respective ideologies does not meet voter expectation. No matter the consequences, parties have stuck with their ideological foundations and are ready to face whatever the consequences are regarding their policy development and implementation. Within these clearly distinguishable party ideologies, both parties try as much as possible to appeal to middle voters (Independent) as well as hard-core Republicans and Democrats. There are instances where red (Republican-leaning) states have voted Democratic in a general election, and there are also instances where blue (Democratic-leaning) states have voted Republican. This is a clear indication that not only are voters paying attention to these ideological stances, but they also pay attention to how these policies affect their daily life.

Clear ideological differences have been healthy for democratic consolidation in Europe and North America. However that is not the case in Africa. Since independence, African political parties and/or states have been tinkering with some ideological stances. This has included both political and economic ideological leanings. These ideologies include African nationalism, African socialism, and scientific socialism.

Nationalism

Nationalism was the mobilizing element for Africa's independence. So for many African states, the ideology of governing parties has been nationalistic in nature. At the early stages, it is understandable to demonstrate the need to bond together with the hope of eliminating any traces of imperialism from the just-liberated, colonial state. Thus in states like Libya (1951), Morocco (1956), Sudan (1956), Tunisia (1956), Ghana (1957), and Guinea (1958), the tendency had been to implement nationalistic policies to nurture the young, independent state. Nationalism is the desire to stick together irrespective of what the outcome might be. However, even though there might be a broader goal, members of a society are also interested in the benefits that these broader goals bring.

African nationalism was formed out of necessity. Rival ethnic groups and other social forces preferred anything other than the continuous presence of white domination and colonialism. Thus African nationalism derived from exogenous sources. Since unity was critical to domestic security in newly independent African states, leaders try as much as possible to implicitly or explicitly exploit African nationalism as a means of rallying the people around a nationalistic cause for domestic stability in postindependence Africa. Mwalimu Julius K. Nyerere even once noted that there cannot be any room for divisions and differences in the newly independent Tanganyika (Nyerere, 1961, p. 199). The implication here is that any means possible should be employed to make the people of Tanganyika, and by extension African societies, look like they are one in order to root out colonialism and its legacies. This kind of nationalism is fundamentally flawed since it rejects the possibility of alternate ways to govern, as well as suppressing and marginalizing those who offer such alternatives.

On a positive note, nationalism as an ideological basis for governing the newly independent states of Africa provided a structure for state organization and effective mobilization and use of resources. In Tanzania, the twin goal of national unity and economic development was put under the umbrella of *Ujamaa* (familyhood). This two-pronged nationalistic goal was expedient for Tanzania at the time. With about 120 different ethnicities and domestic racial diversities it was only prudent that Nyerere emphasize unity as a key interlocking factor in the young country. Also worth noting is that the Tanzanian state and society has benefited from this national unity goal at least in the short term in the area of economics, and in the long term in the area of politics. Tanzania remains one of the few African countries that has somehow been insulated from intense ethnic conflict after independence.

On the economic side Tanzania, with fewer natural resources, also needed a coalescing policy to link its available resources. Agriculture was the only resource available for the country to exploit. By moving from traditionally subsistence-level production to a collective and modern expansion of agriculture, the Tanzanian people stood to benefit from the increased agriculture production.[2] There were however challenges as most of the collective *Ujamaa* villages failed. The people were committed first to their respective subsistence holdings before any attention was given to the collective holdings of the *Ujamaa* ideology.

It is clear from people's behavior that fundamental societal values need to be taken into consideration before crafting broad national policies. Land in contemporary Africa is not just composed of the physical expanse of acres or hectares, but also the traditional beliefs regarding the concept of land itself. People hold individual respect for the land because of the belief that the ancestors have bequeathed the land to them and that they need to administer that piece of land in a way sacred only to themselves. This expatiates on the argument made earlier in this book that Africa's institution building and sustainability cannot ignore the existing traditional institutions that have sustained the society from time immemorial.

Ujamaa in Tanzania also highlights the power of government to develop comprehensive policies shrouded in ideology and to provide a long-term strategy for moving the state forward. Though *Ujamaa* as an ideology may have been analyzed as a failure regarding its overall impact on Tanzania's postindependence economy, it stresses the role of government and political elites in committing themselves to identifiable policy propositions and consequent outcomes. Not only are the electorate given clear options with regard to what to expect, but the governing party also becomes obliged to appropriately defend the means in achieving the policy promises made in the campaign platform.

Other African leaders have had their own interpretation of the importance of ideology in society. Samora Machel of Mozambique once noted,

> Ideology is always the result of a people's concrete revolutionary struggle; for this ideology to become real, it must be accepted and internalized by the broad masses; this is when theory is reborn and becomes

embodied in the process of the daily struggle. This is the only way in which ideology is transformed into an irresistible material force that allows the people to overthrow the older order and to build the new society. (Machel, 1980)[3]

The acceptance and internalization of ideology as explained by Machel is significant in the sense that it highlights the importance of existing institutions in the overall formation of ideology.

As a result of Machel's recognition of the importance of grassroots mobilization, as of 1977 there were 894 "Peoples Assemblies" grassroots mobilization at the local, district, municipal, provincial, and national levels. Machel's policy of the importance of grassroots mobilization unequivocally reflects his ideological stance. Machel's policy of even encouraging direct democracy could be seen where names of candidates contesting the 1977 elections were subjected to public scrutiny and villages were called to comment on whether or not the candidates had the right qualification and attitude to be public officials.[4] Machel's grassroots democracy was not just in mere words but also was backed by actions that link policies to outcomes.

African socialism

Populist socialism was a prominent ideological tool for many postindependence African regimes in the 1960s. This includes states like Ghana, Guinea, Guinea-Bissau, and Mali. In Crawford Young's analysis of this ideology, he noted that though these states espouse socialism[5] they ultimately do not emphasize or embrace Marxism (Young, 1982, p. 12). Crawford Young identified five pillars of populist socialism. These include radical nationalism, a radical mood, anticapitalism, involvement of the peasantry, and the application of moderate levels of socialism (Young, 1982, pp. 100–103). Nkrumah's strong belief in political independence as a panacea to Africa's economic independence to a very large extent shaped his ideological beliefs in postindependence Ghana (Nkrumah, 1962, p. xv). Nkrumah held a belief that, for any meaningful progress to be made and to ensure a path to development, African states need to separate themselves from the intimidating colonial past.[6] Other African leaders believed that a revolutionary attitude is necessary to ensure a path to development compatible with Africa's societal realities.

Burkina Faso's Thomas Sankara held a classic example of this form of ideology. Sankara was a nationalist who also cared about the needs of

Burkinabe's poor. His belief in ideology to spearhead Burkina Faso's development is seen at least in his pronouncements, and later the keen interest he showed in women as significant partners in development. Thomas Sankara earned himself a place among distinguished African leaders as his ideological beliefs enabled him to better mobilize the country's resources.

The fact that many immediate postindependence African leaders espoused ideology to guide their policy goals is worth noting, and the absence of clearly defined ideology should be of concern to elites and citizens of African societies. The imperativeness of ideology was critical in the first place to redefine Africa's postindependence state and to give it a unique nature. It was also meant to structure the effective use of resources both in places where they are limited and in places where such resources are abundant. Thus ideology was seen as a tool for unity and economic development.

The question now is whether ideology has lost its imperativeness within African societies. The lack of interest shown by contemporary African elite regarding ideology in Africa's politics and economy, and the subsequent lack of long-term direction with regard to policy objectives stresses the need for new discussions regarding the role of ideology in African societies. Nkrumah for instance viewed ideology and practice as inextricably linked one with the other. Nkrumah argued that "practice without thought is blind; thought without practice is empty" (Nkrumah, 1964, p. 78). This basically shows that ideology comes with some commitment and the responsibility to transform the expected goals into outcomes.

To stress the importance of ideology, Nkrumah, Sékou Touré of Guinea, and other African leaders believe that ideology should be relevant to domestic realities and institutions. Thus many preferred socialism, with the assumption that Africa's society is a classless society, instead of Marxism, which is fundamentally based on economic class relations within societies. The notion of African socialism—a form of socialism that incorporates Africa's indigenous societal cultures—was shared among several African leaders including Thomas Sankara of Burkina Faso who noted that the Burkinabe revolution was simply based on specific experiences and history of the Burkinabe people (Sethi, 1984, 68). By implication, Sankara was referring to the idea that the practice of socialism may be identical to the Western concept of the term, but in fact the reality was that it is reframed to encapsulate the realities of African societies. Thus he disagreed with the notion that Western societies would like to place Africa's socialist practices in a widely held Western-centric, socialist box.[7]

Scientific Socialism

Other African leaders also experimented with other strands of socialism, including "scientific socialism," which according to Mohamed Siad Barre, fundamentally hinges on the ideas of Marx and Engels (Barre, 1976, p. 26). Scientific socialism, according to Karl Marx and Frederick Engels, is a method for enhancing the understanding and the ability to predict future social, political, and economic developments through the examination of relevant historical trends by the use of the scientific method (Engels, 1880). Engels used this term to describe the social-political-economic theory first pioneered by Marx. Its basis in scientific method may make it a little complex since it is based on theories, observations, and empiricisms determining future outcomes. Since theory is critical to this kind of socialism, it leaves room for changes if key assumptions prove flawed or falsified, thereby allowing practitioners to seek more relevant information within the society to restate the theory in order to make the right predictions.

This type of socialism is complex and challenging for an African setting. The need to have access to reliable data collection and analysis that was unavailable at the time in some of these African states made the understanding and implementation of this form of ideology in Africa a burden. However, some African leaders did not shy away from at least leaning on this ideology as a guide for stability and economic development within their respective states.

Thus during the latter part of the 1970s, we still had African leaders who believed that ideologies not only have intrinsic value, but that they also have extrinsic value that can help structure their political and economic ideas, mobilize support to ensure smooth implementation, and bring about the needed and anticipated change in society. Mohamed Siad Barre of Somalia, Marien Ngouabi's military regime in the Congo-Brazzaville,[8] the Derg era headed by Mengistu Haile Mariam of Ethiopia, Mathieu Kérékou of Benin, and Didier Ratsiraka of Madagascar all espoused scientific socialism. Scientific socialism also received sympathies among revolutionary movements in Zimbabwe, South Africa, and Namibia in the late 1970s.

It is worth mentioning that scientific socialism was in response to African socialism, which has not lived up to its responsibility of establishing stronger states and enhancing economic development within certain states in Africa. Obviously many of the states that practiced African socialism before the late 1970s became riddled with corruption, oppression, and inequality, which made them no different from the conditions that Africans had experienced during colonialism. However, scientific socialism, like its predecessor (African socialism), failed miserably.

All the elements that need to be present for the successful takeoff of scientific socialism as envisaged by Marx and Engels were not present in the African setting. The strong self-conscious working class to lead the revolution was nonexistent (Munslow, 1986, p. 1), and so was the high level of productivity to challenge the capitalist world within the international, political economy.[9] Ethiopia's example serves as a classic case where massive nationalization of businesses and state control of the economy and all means of production did not lead to the achievement of high technologically driven mass productivity envisaged by scientific socialism. Internal ethnic tensions in these countries were inhibiting situations that stifled unity and peace and left no time to concentrate on issues of the economy and development.

CONTEMPORARY STATE OF IDEOLOGY IN AFRICAN SOCIETIES

It is rare these days in Africa to find a political party or state leader associating themselves with any form of ideological leanings as discussed above. However, this has not stopped ideology from being discussed within the African academic space and society. As noted earlier, African intellectuals such as Claude Ake, in discussing the state in Africa, argued that Europeans imposed the nature of contemporary African states on the African people and society (Ake, 1996), 7). Thus the nature of African states does not reflect the realities of African values and culture. The resulting institutional weaknesses that ensued from this imposition led to African political elites preoccupied with how to stabilize their respective states. This strategy to stabilize the states, however, proved counterproductive.

In the process of achieving stable societies, state institutions such as the justice system, military, and police were used to oppress and/or marginalize the very people the state is supposed to protect. Ake notes that apart from the unfortunate fact of African political elites adopting West-ern political structures, including the African state itself, the critical issue of economic development has not even had the opportunity to be on the agenda, and that explains part of the reason for the underdevelopment in Africa. Elites are too busy battling each other for control of the state. Again, the elites have used the state to appropriate state resources for their personal gains. Thus whoever controls the state controls its re-sources.

Ake notes, however, that ideology is still fundamental to liberty and development of Africa due to the commitment that state leaders place on their espoused ideologies. To achieve the goal of a true independent Afri-ca that respects its people, an ideological foundation that takes into con-siderations Africa's traditional institutions is imperative. Ake sums up with the fact that ideological leanings have strong tendencies to focus and achieve results since resources are effectively managed.

IDEOLOGY AND DEMOCRATIC CONSOLIDATION

Ideology has a significant role to play in contemporary Africa's quest for institution building and democratic consolidation. This is because in ad-dition to setting a framework for action, ideology also imposes a burden of commitment to a policy strategy. Due to a lack of ideological leanings of political parties and government policy, strategies have received less commitment and have subsequently affected nation building.

Political parties in Africa may have assumed themselves as either left-leaning or right-leaning. However their policy strategies for achieving goals have mainly consisted of all-of-the-above strategy focusing on the outcome instead of the means or the ideology that drive the commitment to policy outcomes. Thus political parties, and by extension government policy strategy, have been very fluid, ad hoc, and piecemeal. Parties tended to put together patch-work of policies suiting the day to day societal needs instead of long-term strategies. Governments may have between ten and twenty-five-year development plans. In this case, they may be seen as trying to deal with the critical issues that people face. However, most of these plans are clearly unattainable due to the lack of commitment. In addition the lack of a clearly stated ideology creates uncertainties for the political elites. Why would elites prefer to create uncertainties in the way they govern? Being rational decision makers, such uncertainties give them more benefits than it cost them. This may be a short-term tactic to hold on to power for the foreseeable future. The long-term effects, however, are devastating to the elites and the society at large. Regarding the elites, they are faced with the "what if" questions such as how they will survive should they lose the election. The fear of, and the possibility that their dismal performance while in office will lead to them losing public trust, leaves a clout on political elites and the only means to a promising future is to hold on to power. The lack of clearly stated ideologies also confuses and weakens the electorate since they, for the most part, are misinformed. Thus even if they want to punish the nonperforming elites they don't have the relevant information to do so.. Elites have mastered the art of convincing the electorates that they understand the situation and that addressing it is their main goal. These are mainly survival tactics applied by the parties so they can survive into the foreseeable future. Elites have also been able to avoid accountability since they present, or at least are seen as trying to resolve, critical, societal needs. They however leave these issues to become perennial.

In conclusion, the lack of ideology in Africa's political discourse has made governments to focus on policy outcomes instead of the means to the outcome. Ten, twenty, or sometimes thirty years development plans have not been attained since they are not backed by strong ideological underpinnings and commitments. As a result institution building is hindered and very little progress has been seen in Africa's political and economic development pursuit. The consequence for democratic consolidation is not encouraging. An apathetic attitude about democracy has increased in Africa's democratic process. Transitioning to democracy has come at a great cost; people lose their life or have their human rights violated in the process. Espousing ideological beliefs is one of the means of committing to institution building and democratic consolidation in Africa.

NOTES

1. For a more complete review see Lawrence O. Bamikole, "Nkrumah and the Triple Heritage Thesis and Development," *Africana Studies in International Journal of Business, Humanities and Technology* 2 (2, March 2012) pp. 68–76; also see Karl Mannheim, *Ideology and Utopia* (London: Routledge and Kegan Paul, 1960).

2. See Julius K. Nyerere, "Africa's Place in the World," in *Symposium on Africa* (Wellesley, MA: Wellesley College, 1960), p. 157; Nyerere, Julius, 1966. *Freedom and*

Unity. London: Oxford University Press, p. 164; Harvey J. Sindima, *Africa's Agenda: The Legacy of Liberalism and Colonialism in the Crisis of African Values* (Westport, CT: Greenwood, 1995), p. 103.

3. Machel, Samora. "Le Processus de la Revolution Democratique Populaire au Mozambique," Reviewed by Victor Pereira Da Rosa in *Canadian Journal of African Studies* Vol. 14, No. 2 (1980), pp. 361–363.

4. See Marina and David Ottaway's insightful piece in *Afrocommunism* New York: Africana Publishing Co. 1981, pp. 71 and 81–83.

5. Espousing socialism probably serves as a means of rejecting the ideological individualism of capitalism and the perception of de-Westernization as a show of complete independence from colonialism.

6. For more on this reading, see Guy Martin, *African Political Thought* (New York: Palgrave Macmillan, 2012).

7. "Sakara, cet Homme qui Derange," Interview, 43.

8. In 1968, Marien Ngouabi became president of the Republic of Congo, but he changed the country's name to the People's Republic of the Congo and declared it as Africa's first Marxist-Leninist state. As a result he created the Congolese Workers' Party (Parti Congolais du Travail, PCT) as the only legal political party in the country.

9. See more discussions on this in Barry Munslow, ed., *Africa: Problems in the Transition to Socialism* (London: Zed Press, 1986), p. 1.

FOUR

Gender Roles in Africa

Traditional versus Contemporary Institutions

Ali A. Mazrui and Francis Wiafe-Amoako

Issues of gender (women) in contemporary times have been viewed either from a moral or economic perspective. While some have noted that de-emphasizing the importance of women's role in society is effectively not making use of a significant amount of societal resources, others have argued from a moral perspective noting that it is just the right (moral) thing to do to include women in all aspects of the society because women have played critical roles in society since time immemorial.

The institutional basis for the change in women's traditional role in society, though acknowledged, has not been explored consistently. This chapter explores the institutional basis of women's role in traditional African societies. It argues that the contemporary role of women in Africa's society, and by extension, worldwide is institutionally driven. Thus it is not the case that suddenly economic and moral imperatives have become so significant as to overlook the tremendous contribution of women in society, but rather that the progressive international and domestic institutions and norms over the years has been the driving force in explaining the change in women's role in African societies.

TRADITIONAL INSTITUTIONS AND EFFECT ON
WOMEN'S ROLE WITHIN AFRICAN SOCIETIES

The traditional role for women in African societies has had tremendous impact on women's participation in politics, the economy, and society. Though these institutional roles are not written, it is clear that generational application of these institutions has shaped the gender dynamics in African societies. Traditional gender institutions have limited women's roles to the domestic arena. However, contemporary institutions in Africa have empowered African women to demand and achieve participation in public decision making.

"In the beginning was man and woman. Their first child was human culture itself." In many traditional African cultures there has been a belief that God made woman the custodian of *fire, water,* and *earth.* God himself took charge of the fourth element of the universe—the omnipresent *air.*[1]

Custody of fire entailed responsibility for making energy available. And the greatest source of energy in rural Africa is still firewood. The African woman became disproportionately responsible for finding and carrying huge bundles of firewood, though quite often it was men who initially chopped down the big trees.

Custody of water involved a liquid that was a symbol of both survival and cleanliness. The African woman became responsible for ensuring that this critical substance was available for the family. She trekked long distances to fetch water. But where a well needed to be dug, it was often the man who did the digging.

The custody of earth has been part of a doctrine of *dual fertility.* Woman ensures the *survival* of this generation by maintaining a central role in cultivation—and preserving the fertility of the *soil.* Woman ensures the *arrival* of the next generation in her role as mother—the fertility of the *womb.* Dual fertility becomes an aspect of the triple custodial role of African womanhood, though always in partnership with the African man.

What has happened to this doctrine of triple custody in the period since the colonial days? Different elements of the colonial experience affected the roles of men and women in Africa in different ways.

Among the factors that increased the woman's role on the land was wage labor for the men. Faced with an African population reluctant to work for low wages for somebody else, colonial rulers had already experimented with both forced labor and taxation as a way of inducing Africans (especially men) to join the colonial workforce.

According to Margaret Jean Hay, wage labor for men took some time before it began to affect women's role on the land. Hay's own work was among Luo women in Kenya.

> By 1930 a large number of men had left Kowe at least once for outside employment. . . . More than half of this group stayed away for periods of fifteen years or more. . . . This growing export of labor from the province might be thought to have increased the burden of agricultural work for women. . . . As early as 1910, administrators lamented the fact that Nyanza was becoming the labor pool of the entire colony. . . . Yet the short-term migrants of the 1920's were usually unmarried youths, who played a relatively minor role in the local economy beyond occasional herding and the conquest of cattle in war. Furthermore, the short-term labor migrants could and often did arrange to be away during the slack periods in the agriculture cycle. . . . Thus labor migration in the period before 1930 actually removed little labor from the local economy and did not significantly alter the sexual division of labor. (Hay, 1976, pp. 98–99)[2]

But Margaret Hay goes on to demonstrate how the Great Depression and the Second World War changed the situation as migrant labor and conscription of males took a bigger and bigger proportion of men away from the land. This was compounded by the growth of mining industries like the gold mining at Kowe from 1934 onward.

> The long-term absence of men had an impact on the sexual division of labor, with women and children assuming a greater share of agricultural work than ever before. . . . The thirties represent a transition with regard to the sexual division of labor, and it was clearly the women who bore the burden of the transition in rural areas. (Hay, 1976, p. 105)

Women in this period, from the 1930s onward, became more deeply involved as "custodians of earth." In southern Africa the migration of men to the mines became even more dramatic. By the 1950s a remarkable bifurcation was taking place in some southern African societies—a division between a male proletariat (industrial working class) and a female peasantry. South Africa's regulations against families joining their husbands at the mines exacerbated this tendency toward *gender apartheid*, the segregation of the sexes. Many women in the Front Line States had to fulfill their triple custodial role of fire, water, and earth in greater isolation than ever.

The wars of liberation in southern Africa from the 1960s took their own toll on family stability and traditional sexual division of labor. Some of the fighters did have their wives with them. Indeed, liberation armies like ZANLA (Zimbabwe African National Liberation Army) and ZIPRA (Zimbabwe People's Revolutionary Army) in Zimbabwe and FRELIMO (Mozambique Liberation Front) in Mozambique included a few female fighters. But on the whole, the impact of the wars disrupted family life and the traditional sexual division of labor.

After independence there were counterrevolutionary wars among some of the Front Line States. The most artificial of the postcolonial wars was that of Mozambique, initiated by the so-called Mozambique National Resistance (MNR or RENAMO). The movement was originally created by reactionary white Rhodesians to punish President Samora Machel for his support for Robert Mugabe's forces in Zimbabwe. After Zimbabwe's independence, the Mozambique National Resistance became a surrogate army for reactionary whites in the Republic of South Africa and committed a variety of acts of sabotage against the fragile postcolonial economy of Mozambique.

Again, there have been implications for relations between the genders. In addition to the usual disruptive consequences of war for the family, by the mid-1980s, the MNR had inflicted enough damage on the infrastructure in Mozambique that many migrant workers never got home to their families in between their contracts with the South African mines. The miners often remained on the border between South Africa and Mozambique, waiting for their next opportunity at the mines, without ever having found transportation to get to their families in distant villages of Mozambique.

It is not completely clear how this situation has affected the doctrine of "dual fertility" in relation to the role of the African woman. One possibility is that the extra-long absences of the husbands have reduced fertility rates in some communities like Mozambique. The other scenario is that the pattern of migrant labor in southern Africa generally has initiated a tendency toward de facto polyandry. The woman who was left behind acquired over time a de facto extra husband. The two husbands took their turn over time with the woman. The migrant laborer from the mines had conjugal priority between mining contracts if he did manage to get to the village. He also had prior claim to the new babies unless agreed otherwise.[3]

If the more widespread pattern is still that of declining fertility as a result of extra-long absences of husbands, the principle of "dual fertility" has reduced the social functions of the fertility of the womb and increased the woman's involvement in matters pertaining to the fertility of the soil. On the other hand, if the more significant tendency in mining communities in southern Africa is toward de facto polyandry, a whole new nexus of social relationships may be in the making in southern Africa.[4]

While women's role on the farm expanded, women's land *rights* did not necessarily improve. The number of female cultivators multiplied, but land continued to be owned by fathers, husbands, brothers or, even more, traditionally, by a clan or tribe, led by male elders.

There is also women's role in the culture of *water*. As "custodian of water," the African woman has played a bigger role than men in fetching water from lakes, rivers, or wells. Women have also utilized a bigger share of the domestic water supply—washing dishes and domestic laundry, cleaning babies, and using water for personal female hygiene.

Ironically, although women have a bigger role than men in the supply and consumption of fresh water, women have a lesser role in the culture of ocean saltwater. Until the 1970s there have been few women sailors since the days of dhows and sailing ships. Naval fleets have been overwhelmingly dominated by men. Men have also predominated in oceanic fisheries. Women have tilled the land; men have tamed the seas. In the words of Harry Belafonte's song about an island in the Caribbean sun:

> I see woman on bended knee
> Cutting cane for the family
> [sugar cane]
> I see man on the water's side
> Casting net at the surging tide
> [fishing net]. (Lyrics published by BMG Rights Management, US, LLC)

To summarize, the African woman is central in the culture of freshwater, but marginal in the careers of the oceans. The African woman is central in agricultural roles, but relatively marginal in agricultural rights. The struggle continues in pursuit of gender justice, and the role of institutions cannot be overemphasized.

THE GENDER OF TECHNOLOGY

Other changes that affected relationships between men and women in Africa during this period include the impact of new technologies on gender roles. Cultivation with the hoe still left the African woman centrally involved in agriculture. But cultivation with the tractor has often been a prescription for male dominance.

> When you see a farmer
> On bended knee
> Tilling land
> For the family
> The chances are
> It is a *she*
>
> When you see tractor
> Passing by
> And the driver
> Waves you "Hi"
> The chances are
> It is a *he*! (Mazrui, 1998)

Mechanization of agriculture in Africa has tended to marginalize women. Their role as "custodians of earth" is threatened by male prerogatives in new and more advanced technologies. It is true that greater male involvement in agriculture could help reduce the heavy burdens of work undertaken by women on the land. On the other hand, there is no reason why this relief in workload for women should not come through better technology. Tractors were not invented to be driven solely by men.

Another threat to the central role of African women in the economy in this period has come from the nature of Western education. It is true that the Westernized African woman is usually more mobile and has more freedom for her own interests than is her traditional sister. But a transition from custodian of fire, water, and earth to keeper of the typewriter is definitely a form of marginalization for African womanhood. Typing is less fundamental for survival than cultivation. Since the second half of the twentieth century, the Westernized African woman has tended to be more free but less important for African economies than the traditional woman in rural areas.

The third threat to the role of the African woman in this period has come with the internationalization of African economies. When economic activity in Africa was more localized, women had a decisive role in local markets and as traders. But the colonial and postcolonial tendencies toward enlargement of economic scale have increasingly pushed women to the side in international decision making. It is true that Nigerian women especially have refused to be completely marginalized even in international trade. A Nigerian woman has risen almost to the top of the World Bank. But on the whole, the Africans who deal with international markets and sit on the boards of transnational corporations are overwhelmingly men. At the meetings of the Organization of Petroleum Exporting Countries (OPEC)—where Muslims predominate—there are additional cultural inhibitions about having even Nigeria represented by a female delegate.

POLICY IMPLICATIONS FOR WOMEN ENTREPRENEURS

What are the policy implications of all these trends? One central imperative is indeed to arrest the marginalization of women and to cultivate further their entrepreneurial potential. *Cultural adjustment* is the imperative.

Women as custodians of earth had traditionally emphasized food cultivation. But from now on, greater involvement of women in the production of cash crops for export is one way of linking tradition to modernity—and preventing Africa's economic internationalization from resulting in the marginalization of African women.

But support for traditional market women in food production and local trade need not suffer as a result of the new androgynization of cash-crop production. Credit facilities should be made available in such a manner that equity exists not only between men and women, but also between Westernized and non-Westernized females. As matters now stand, traditionalist non-Westernized women are often at a disadvantage when assessed for credit worthiness.

On the other hand, a higher proportion of non-Westernized women are involved in agricultural production than are their Westernized women. Indeed, cultural Westernization of women—though improving their credit worthiness—tends to decrease women's direct economic productivity. A balance has to be struck between the two categories of women (Westernized and non-Westernized) in relation to both credit and production.

Preventing technology from marginalizing women is yet another imperative. Special programs for women in technical training—from driving tractors to repairing a truck engine—should be inaugurated. It will not happen on its own. Such shifts in the cultural aspects of technology need to be addressed purposefully. Effective participation of women in the world of economic entrepreneurship requires their upliftment in the world of technical and mechanical skills as well.

Women as custodians of fire make them the greatest users of firewood on the continent. But shouldn't women also be centrally involved in forest management and reforestation? Wood should increasingly be approached as an integrated industry, sensitized to the needs of environmental protection and ecological balance. Women as the greatest users of firewood should also become among the leading planters of trees for reforestation. The late Wangari Maathai led the way in mobilizing women to plant millions of trees.

This would not be incompatible with women's involvement in the commercial aspects of wood more generally. Carpentry and furniture making are crafts that cry out for much greater female involvement than has been achieved so far. Culturally women are often the selectors of furniture and the trustees of the domestic infrastructure of the family. And yet it is an anomaly that African women have played such a limited role in designing furniture or making it. This is an area of entrepreneurship that beckons the female participant to become more involved.

As traditional custodians of water, do women have any special role in this era of faucets and dams? Africa's women, as we indicated, still trek long distances in some rural areas for their water. But water-related industries are surprisingly still male dominated. This includes the whole infrastructure of water supply in urban areas. Even commercialized laundry and dry cleaning for the elite and for foreigners in African towns is still usually owned and managed by men, even when women do most of the washing and ironing. The soap manufacturing industry is also male owned and male managed, even when the consumers are overwhelmingly women. One question that arises is whether these water-related industries are appropriate areas of linking tradition to modernity in Africa's gender roles.

What is at stake is the tapping of female talent where it was previously underutilized. What is at stake is also the androgynization of entrepreneurship. Once again the imperative is *cultural adjustment* in the form of domestic institutional building or adopting compatible foreign institutions.

Can the traditional custodian of fire be the innovative consumer of hydroelectric power? Can the traditional trustee of water be the new creative user of the high dam? Can the traditional trustee of earth take control of a new (and more creative) green revolution?

The future of the continent depends upon a new sexual equation in the whole economic process. The future of the continent depends more fundamentally on a *cultural*, rather than on a structural, adjustment. In 2012 a Nigerian female minister of finance was nearly elected president of the World Bank in Washington, D.C.

But none of those measures of culture adjustment regarding gender would be feasible without a pronounced role by the state. Classical privatization and laissez-faire would simply permit worsening conditions of marginalization for women. Progress toward female entrepreneurialization would be aborted or retarded. This is one reason why the cause of androgynous entrepreneurship in Africa needs an activist and enlightened state. The economy under such intervention would become less private—but the market could be released from some of the shackles of tradition and cultural prejudice.

Traditional and cultural beliefs are part of domestic institutions that have shaped women's role and in some cases discriminated against the full potential of African women. As noted in chapter 1, institutions shape behavior and relationships and are to a greater extent, legitimized. Though many may view discrimination against women enforced by the application of traditional institutions within African societies unproductive, in most instances the legitimacy of such institutions paralyzed attempts by progressive-minded individuals to alter these institutions. However, as a result of globalization and increased levels of education, foreign institutions are gradually integrated into African societies. These institutions have tremendously impacted the role of women in African societies, and that role is gradually being enhanced by gender-friendly institutions. Some of these new institutions include international norms, such as UN Conventions on Women and the wave of democratization on the African continent.

CONTEMPORARY INSTITUTIONS AND THEIR EFFECT ON
WOMEN'S ROLE IN AFRICAN SOCIETIES

In contemporary times there has been a shift from traditional institutions that impact women's role within African societies. More and more women have found opportunities within the public space that make them play a leadership role as opposed to the era where institutions limited women's role to maintaining the domestic arena and supporting subsistence economy within African societies. This can be seen in the increase in women's participation in the political arena and also advocacy movement organizations.

The situation in Africa is not an isolated case. Many women outside of Africa, both in developed and developing states, are experiencing a significant wave of participation in the public arena leading to gender social change. However, these waves should not be seen as a newfound love regarding the essence of women's participation in the areas of politics, the economy, and society. Changes in women's participation must be viewed within the context of progressive and emerging institutions. Those changes have come as a result of consistent piecemeal institutional changes both within and outside of Africa.

The post-1990s has seen increased women's participation in politics and leadership. Rwanda continues to witness the highest increase in the number of women in its legislature, with several other African states in the range of 30 percent and up. According to data compiled by Inter-Parliamentary Union,[5] "Women in National Parliaments" (see table 4.1), there are six African states in the first twenty countries with high percentage of women in the legislature. The African countries include Rwanda (63.8 percent), Senegal (42.7 percent), South Africa (41.5 percent), Namibia (41.3 percent), Mozambique (39.6 percent), and Angola (36.8 percent). In seven other African countries, more that 30 percent of representatives in the legislature are women. They include Tanzania (36 percent), Uganda (35 percent), Algeria (31.6 percent), Zimbabwe (31.5 percent), Tunisia (31.3 percent), Cameroon (31.1 percent), and Burundi (30.5 percent). Some of the factors that have contributed in this change of traditional role of Africa women include the changing nature of domestic political dynamics, the rise in women's movements, and the realization by women that their specific needs are not necessarily met when the overall statewide needs or goals are achieved.

Rank	Country	Elections	Seats	Women	% W	Elections	Seats	Women	% Women
1	Rwanda	9 2013	80	51	63.8%	9 2011	26	10	38.5%
5	Seychelles	9 2011	32	14	43.8%				
7	Senegal	7 2012	150	64	42.7%				
10	South Africa	5 2014	400	166	41.5%	5 2014	54	19	35.2%
11	Namibia	11 2014	104	43	41.3%	11 2010	26	6	23.1%
13	Mozambique	10 2014	250	99	39.6%				
19	Angola	8 2012	220	81	36.8%				
23	Tanzania	10 2010	350	126	36%				
24	Uganda	2 2011	386	135	35%				
27	Algeria	5 2012	462	146	31.3%	12 2012	144	10	6.9%
28	Zimbabwe	7 2013	270	85	31.5%	7 2013	80	38	47.5%
30	Tunisia	10 2014	217	68	31.3%				
31	Cameroon	9 2013	180	56	31.1%	4 2013	100	20	20%
34	Burundi	7 2010	105	32	30.5%	7 2010	41	19	46.3%
38	Ethiopia	5 2010	547	152	27.8%	5 2010	135	22	16.3%
43	Lesotho	5 2012	120	32	26.7%	6 2012	33	9	27.3%
44	South Sudan	8 2011	332	88	26.5%	8 2011	50	5	10%
48	Mauritania	11 2013	147	37	25.2%	11 2009	56	8	14.3%
50	Sudan	4 2010	354	86	24.3%	5 2010	29	5	17.2%
52	Equatorial Guinea	5 2013	100	24	24%	5 2013	73	10	13.7%
60	Eritrea	2 1994	150	33	22%				
61	Guinea	9 2013	114	25	21.9%				
63	Cabo Verde	2 2011	72	15	20.8%				
65	Madagascar	12 2013	151	31	20.5%				
71	Kenya	3 2013	350	69	19.7%	3 2013	68	18	26.5%

Rank	Country	Elections	Seats	Women	% W	Elections	Seats	Women	% Women
76	Sao Tome and Principe	10 2014	55	10	18.2%				
78	Togo	7 2013	91	16	17.6%				
82	Morocco	11 2011	395	67	17%	10 2009	270	6	2.2%
84	Malawi	5 2014	192	32	16.7%				
86	Libya	6 2014	188	30	16%				
90	Chad	2 2011	188	28	14.9%				
92	Gabon	12 2011	120	17	14.2%	12 2014	102	19	18.6%
94	Somalia	8 2012	275	38	13.8%				
95	Guinea-Bissau	4 2014	102	14	13.7%				
97	Burkina Faso	11 2014	90	12	13.3%				
97	Niger	1 2011	113	15	13.3%				
102	Djibouti	2 2013	55	7	12.7%				
102	Zambia	9 2011	158	20	12.7%				
104	Sierra Leone	11 2012	121	15	12.4%				
107	Mauritius	12 2014	69	8	11.6%				
110	Liberia	10 2011	73	8	11%	12 2014	30	3	10%
111	Ghana	12 2012	275	30	10.9%				
115	Botswana	10 2014	63	6	9.5%				
115	Mali	11 2013	147	14	9.5%				
116	Gambia	3 2012	53	5	9.4%				
119	Democratic Republic of the Congo	11 2011	492	44	8.9%	1 2007	108	5	4.6%
122	Benin	4 2011	83	7	8.4%				
124	Congo	7 2012	136	10	7.4%	10 2014	72	14	19.4%
125	Nigeria	4 2011	360	24	6.7%	4 2011	109	7	6.4%
126	Swaziland	9 2013	65	4	6.3%	10 2010	215	4	1.8%

THE CHANGING NATURE OF OVERALL
DOMESTIC POLITICAL DYNAMICS

The political system, as an institution, structures behaviors within states. These institutions can be in the form of regime type, judicial systems, and laws that distinguishes one state from the other. In Africa, regime types negotiate the question regarding what practical system is appropriate for stability. Most countries in Africa have tinkered with single-party political systems in which the ruling government promulgates laws to discourage activities of multipartyism. Kwame Nkrumah, the first president of Ghana, remarked when he argued for a single-party state, that African societies are so divided that multiparty systems would practically weaken the newly independent Ghana. The same conclusion advocating for a single-party state was made by Mwalimu Julius K. Nyerere of Tanzania when, in order to discourage any relevance for multiparty system, he argued that African societies are united or classless. Houphouët-Boigny of La Côte D'Ivoire noted that his country was a single-party state because there was simply no opposition party available. Still others such as Sékou Touré of Guinea argued for an ideological underpinning for a single-party system.

The underlying assumption of a single-party system is that unity is more important that varied opinions exhibited by strong opposition. Alongside the single-party state, an explosion of military governments in the two decades of Africa's independence stifled efforts at creating an environment conducive for women's involvement in political decision making. The judiciary during these periods merely existed by name and just served as a tool for entrenching the preferences of the elite. Institutions that encouraged free participation were nonexistent. Other state institutions such as the police and the military were at the behest of the political elites and operated as intimidating and oppressive instruments of the state.

Some scholars have referred to the 1960s through the 1980s as periods in which African states acted as "Frankenstein" states as helpless citizens who participated in the independence struggle had to grapple with the dictatorial nature of the state that emerged after independence.[6] Sustainable institutions were discouraged, as were any efforts at trying to ensure women's participation in the political process.

Even where democratic principles and freedoms are entrenched within the system, women's needs have either been subsumed under much larger goals, or simply suppressed. A case example is in the United States when, after the ratification of the Reconstruction Amendments (Thirteenth [1865], Fourteenth [1868], and Fifteenth [1870] Amendments), women still had difficulties in exercising their full franchise rights under what the law had provided. After the Fifteenth Amendment was adopted, which authorized states not to deny citizens the right to vote, Virginia Minor of Missouri attempted to exercise her franchise in 1872 and was denied. The case eventually ended up in the U.S. Supreme Court. In the famous 1875 case of *Minor v. Happersett*, the U.S. Supreme Court argued that the Privileges and Immunities Clause under the Fourteenth Amendment does not guarantee a person's [a woman's] right to vote.

It took the Nineteenth Amendment to the U.S. Constitution that was ratified in 1920 for a woman in America to be able to vote. The Nineteenth Amendment, which overruled the Supreme Court decision on *Minor v. Happersett*, literally states that a person's right to vote could not be denied based on the sex of the person. In all, it took fifty good years after the ratification of the Fifteenth Amendment before a woman can vote. Again it has to take another forty-five years before laws could be passed to end all forms of voting discriminations against minorities. The Voting Rights Act of 1965 did just that.

Even within the broader civil rights struggle in the United States, the achievement of certain civil rights freedoms for African Americans and women did not necessarily lead to women's rising to top-level leadership and other public decision-making spaces. These sentiments were expressed by prominent African American women such as Dorothy I. Heights who was frustrated that a united council—the Council of United Civil Rights Leadership (CUCRL)—formed to unify civil rights organization in the 1960s and to support the March on Washington, was just not ready to listen to concerns raised by women as part of this unified group.[7] The extent of African American women's vulnerability is clearly depicted here when their own African American men would not afford them a role in the public space.

These African American women's situation is not an isolated one. Many women's organizations that were formed in Africa during the independence struggle to the middle of the 1980s were merely part of a greater national cause. In Zimbabwe and Algeria, women's participation in the independence struggle was seen as significant and therefore nationalist. However women's participation in the independence struggle in other African countries were seen as part of a broader nationalist cause—independence. The assumption here is that when the "full cake" of independence is achieved, women by default would not be left out and would have their share of the "cake," including their appropriate role in leadership and decision making.[8] Thus in states such as Mozambique and Guinea-Bissau, women's participation in independence was considered a critical part of their moral responsibility to help liberate the country from the Portuguese colonial rule (Ranchod-Nilson, 2006; Urdang 1978). For example, the women's movement in Mozambique had a strong attachment to FRELIMO to an extent that it dared not speak against the party's gender policies that were unfavorable to women (Casimiro 1986; 1999).

In most cases women's organizations were being co-opted by the ruling or opposition parties, thereby diluting the true independence and organization of women's movement formation. Women's group co-optation was prevalent in many postindependence African states, and the situation worsened when most of these states ended up as single-party states and military regimes. As a result women empowerment and their abilities to compete in political leadership and decision making were curtailed during this period.

THE RISE IN WOMEN'S SOCIAL MOVEMENTS

The rise of women's social movements is a fundamental linchpin to true women liberation and independence. Women finally get to push for a role in public decision making and influence as opposed to their assigned roles as homemakers and preoccupied with very microdevelopmental issues such as needing the construction of day cares, market stalls, access to farms lands, and living in the shadows of men. If women are to make a greater impact and change the processes that shape their lives in society, their competitive involvement and engagement in the political space is imperative. Strong and viable women's social movements become fundamental.

This rise in women's social movements came as a result of changes in both international and regional norms that promoted women's involvement in political decision making, the availability of external funding to support women's movement formation, the wave of democratization and political liberalization, and the improved education and skills of African women. Thus, the middle of the 1980s through the 1990s became critical in women's rise to power and competitive engagement in the political space within Africa.

International and Regional Conferences and Norms

Prior to the influential Beijing conference in 1995, earlier UN conferences on women had laid the institutional foundations for women empowerment and advancement. In 1975, the first UN women's conference in Mexico City was attended by 133 governments and about 6,000 representatives from nongovernmental organizations (NGOs). This conference laid the foundational framework for the advancement of women status within states by putting in place a World Plan of Action for the implementation of the objectives of the International Women's Year. Portions of the Mexico City declaration on women's empowerment state as follows:

> *Aware* that the problems of women, who constitute half of the world's population, are the problems of society as a whole, and that changes in the present economic, political and social situation of women must become an integral part of efforts to transform the structures and attitudes that hinder the genuine satisfaction of their needs, . . .
> *Taking into account* the role played by women in the history of humanity, especially in the struggle for national liberation, the strengthening of international peace, and the elimination of imperialism, colonialism, neo-colonialism, foreign occupation, zionism, alien domination, racism and apartheid;
> *Stressing* that greater and equal participation of women at all levels of decision making shall decisively contribute to accelerating the pace of development and the maintenance of peace;
> *Stressing* also that women and men of all countries should have equal rights and duties and that it is the task of all States to create the necessary conditions for the attainment and the exercise thereof;
> *Recognizing* that women of the entire world, whatever differences exist between them, share the painful experience of receiving or having received unequal treatment, and that as their awareness of this phenomenon increases they will become natural allies in the struggle against any form of oppression, such as is practiced under colonialism, neo-colonialism, zionism, racial discrimination, and apartheid, thereby

constituting an enormous revolutionary potential for economic and social change in the world today;

Recognizing that changes in the social and economic structure of
societies, even though they are among the prerequisites, cannot of
themselves ensure an immediate improvement in the status of a group
which has long been disadvantaged, and that urgent consideration
must therefore be given to the full, immediate and early integration of
women into national and international life;

Emphasizing that under-development imposes upon women a dou-
ble burden of exploitation, which must be rapidly eliminated, and that
full implementation of national development policies designed to fulfill
this objective is seriously hindered by the existing inequitable system
of international economic relations, . . .

Decides to promulgate the following principles:

1. Equality between women and men means equality in their dignity and worth as human beings as well as equality in their rights,
opportunities and responsibilities.[9]

With specific reference to Africa, the Mexico City conference noted the
essence of research and training for the advancement of women in Africa.
It stated:[10]

> Considering the increasingly important role of African women in
> the political, economic, social and cultural affairs of their coun-
> tries;
>
> Considering the need to establish all the conditions required for
> education, training and the elimination of illiteracy in order to
> ensure more effective participation of African women;
>
> Considering the precarious situation of the great majority of wom-
> en in Africa and the consequent need for vigorous and compre-
> hensive action;
>
> Considering the objectives of the Pan-African Women's Organiza-
> tion relating to the acceleration of the advancement of African
> women;
>
> Considering the decision of the Pan-African Women's Organization
> to establish training Centre at the organization's headquarters;
>
> Welcomes the decision of the ECA Conference of African Ministers
> at Nairobi to establish an African Training and Research Centre
> for Women (resolution 269 (XII)) of the Economic Commission
> for Africa, of 28 February 1975.

For African women, the UN Conference on Women held in Nairobi in
1985 was the turning point in getting them the necessary motivations for
pushing for equality regarding their participation in national decision

making and in things that concern women. From an institutional point of view it is important to note that these two women's conferences also drew on international documents that espouse equality of all humankind. This includes the UN Charter and the Universal Declaration of Human Rights (UDHR), which espouses equality. The Nairobi conference had a tremendous impact on women's movement organizations in Africa, especially in East African states such as Kenya, Tanzania, and Uganda.[11] The conference attracted about 1,900 delegates from 157 member states. State governments that had adopted the strategies and measures arrived at the Nairobi conference to pursue and achieve gender equality at the national level, as well as the promotion of women's participation in the areas of development and peace.

Regarding women's role in peace and conflict in Africa, the African Centre for the Constructive Resolution of Disputes (ACCORD), a civil society organization based in South Africa, works to find creative African solutions to the challenges that conflict brings to the continent. ACCORD also champions the importance of including African women in peace processes. In May 2012, ACCORD organized an African Women Mediators Seminar in Johannesburg, South Africa, under its Peacemaking Unit's African Union (AU) Mediation Support Capacity Project and in collaboration with the AU Peace and Security Department. The two-day seminar brought together policy makers, high level practitioners, political leaders, and people from academia to discuss African women's role in mediation and the peace process on the continent. Some of the participants who shared their experiences at the seminar included Betty Bigombe, a minister from Uganda, and Lindiwe Zulu, an ambassador from South Africa, with the keynote address delivered by Mrs. Graça Machel, chairperson of ACCORD's Board of Trustees.[12]

Again, the United Nations Security Council Resolution 1325 (2000) notes the relevance of gender in conflict prevention and peace building. It reaffirms "the important role of women in the prevention and resolution of conflicts and in peace-building, and *stressing* the importance of their equal participation and full involvement in all efforts for the maintenance and promotion of peace and security, and the need to increase their role in decision making with regard to conflict prevention and resolution."[13]

It is also important to mention the extent to which international norms have given legitimacy and power to individual women to lead women's group conflict resolution and peace building. Leymah Gbowee led a group of Liberian women to form an organization called "Women of Liberia Mass Action for Peace." This organization was able to force a meeting with then-president Charles Taylor at the height of the second Liberian Civil War, and also obtained a promise from Taylor to attend peace talks in Ghana. Again, the women's group traveled all the way to Accra, the capital of Ghana and engaged in nonviolent protests during the peace process to bring pressure on the warring factions to consider a quick peace agreement. They also staged a silent protest outside of Liberia's Presidential Palace when the peace talk appeared to be stalling.

The Fourth UN Conference on Women in Beijing in 1995 was symbolic, especially when it was held in a Communist and male-dominated Chinese society. It was a turning point in the global agenda to push for women's equality. The Chinese government's acceptance to hold this conference on its soil was a major breakthrough for women. It sent out the message that the glass ceiling could potentially crack in patriarchal societies to allow women's independence and participation in national leadership. Though there has never been a woman at the top tier level of power in the Central Committee of the Chinese Communist Party (CCCCP), Chinese women have gradually been increasing their participation at the National People's Congress of China (NPPC) with their numbers increasing from 12 percent in 1954 to 21.3 percent in 2008. In addition to that, women's participation in the Standing Committee has risen from 5 percent in 1954 to 16.6 percent in 2008. The implementation of quotas by the Chinese government has resulted in women taking leadership roles in several government departments. It is also estimated that women occupy deputy governor positions in about 87 percent provincial governments as of 2010.[14] Though women's visible role in the international arena is not as we would expect, comparative to other states, there is no doubt that Chinese women are making a greater impact in public decision making. However, Chinese women's dominant role in the socioeconomic life in China cannot be overemphasized. With the Chinese economy being the second largest in the world, and women playing a dominant role, there is much optimism that this trend would only impact positively on women's role in the CCCCP in the foreseeable future. Thus the international awareness created as a result of the Beijing Conference has at least held off any possibility that the Chinese government may develop legislations to inhibit women's empowerment and advancement within the Chinese society.

Again, the Beijing Declaration and the Platform for Action that was unanimously adopted by 189 countries was a key document that opened the floodgate for global women empowerment. In addition to certain critical areas that enhanced women's development contained in the Declaration such as women and health, violence against women, women and poverty, human rights for women, the education and training of women, women [potential] involvement in contemporary armed conflict, women and the media, and the girl child, the Declaration also dealt with issues of equality of women participation in political power and decision making, and pragmatic institutional mechanisms for advancing the cause of women. The Beijing conference, like UN Women conferences, built on previous conferences that over the years have gradually been accepted, at least in principle, by states. These declarations have thus become institutionalized, and acted as the force behind the growing expansion of women involvement in societal decision making at the regional, national, and local levels. In Africa, these institutions have contributed immensely in helping with the establishment of numerous effective women's organizations, thereby helping to move women from their traditionally assigned domestic roles as keepers of the homes to participating in local and national roles and responsibilities in helping to effectively develop and implement policies that enhance women empowerment.

NOTES

1. I (Ali A. Mazrui) am indebted to the late Okot p'Bitek, the Ugandan anthropologist and poet for information about myths of womanhood in Northern Uganda. Okot and I also discussed similarities and differences between African concepts of matter and ideas of Empedocles, the Greek philosopher of the fifth century BCE. Consult also Okot p'Bitek, *African Religions in Western Scholarship* (Nairobi: East African Literature Bureau, 1971).

2. For a feminist perspective consult also Maria Rosa Cutrufelli, *Women of Africa: Roots of Oppression* (London: Zed Press, 1983).

3. There is no doubt such arrangements occur in Mozambique. What is not clear is how widespread de facto polyandry is becoming in southern Africa.

4. I (Ali A. Mazrui) am the one speaking and I am indebted to the field research and interviews in southern Africa which accompanied the BBC/WETA television project, *The Africans: A Triple Heritage* (1985–1986). I am also grateful to the work associated with volume 8 of the UNESCO *General History of Africa* (edited by Ali A. Mazrui).

5. Data available at http://www.ipu.org/wmn-e/classif.htm. This was accessed on March 28, 2015, and includes the data available as at February 1, 2015. The site updates data regularly.

6. See Ali A. Mazrui's 2002, "The Frankenstein State and the Internal Order," in *Africa and Other Civilizations: Conquest and Counter-Conquest*, eds. Ricardo René Laremont and Fouad Kalouche (Trenton, NJ: Africa World Press).

7. See Bettye Collier-Thomas and V. P. Franklin, *Sisters in the Struggle: African American Women in the Civil Rights—Black Power Movements* (New York: New York University Press, 2001), pp. 81–94.

8. This is somewhat in line with what is attributed to Kwame Nkrumah, Ghana's first president, that "seek ye first the political freedom and all other things shall be added to you."

9. See http://www.un-documents.net/mex-dec.htm .

10. See http://www.unorg/womenwatch/daw/beijing/otherconferences/mexico/mexico%20section%20III.pdf

11. For more information on this, see Alli M. Tripp et al., *African Women's Movements: Changing Political Landscape* (New York: Cambridge University Press, 2009).

12. For additional information on ACCORD, see http://www.accord.org.za.

13. United Nations Security Council (SC) Resolution 1325 (2000) is available at http://www.un.org/womenwatch/ods/S-RES-1325(2000)-E.pdf.

14. See Benxiang Zeng, "Women Political Participation in China: Improved or Not," *Journal of International Women's Studies* 15 (January 1, 2014).

FIVE

Legitimacy and Rule

Africa in Search of a Political Order

Francis Wiafe-Amoako

Legitimacy[1] permeates every facet of human interaction. In politics, social, and economic relations legitimacy plays a key role in substantiating those relations. In African societies legitimacy is accorded a special place. Traditional systems continue to influence contemporary societal relationship. From family, clan, kinship, and chieftaincy levels, legitimacy plays an influential role, and will continue into the foreseeable future.

Legitimacy has been one of the potential underlying factors of conflicts within societies and to a greater extent, the entire state. However, less attention has been given to the issue of legitimacy of the African state, its government and institutions. This chapter identifies two issues of legitimacy within African states that need attention. These are the legitimacy of the African state itself, and the legitimacy of the political institutions that currently exist within those states.

The legitimacy of the African state itself is beyond the discussion of this chapter. African leaders at independence did not see the imperativeness of visiting the nature of the postcolonial state within the context of the nation-state and the stability of the newly independent states. Critical among these is the boundaries of those states that were demarcated by economic imperatives during the colonial era. The current African Union Border Program (AUBP) is a step in the right direction. However, the discussion needs to go beyond the reconceptualization of borders as bridges to a strategy of building viable nation-states. Thus, the issue of the legitimacy of the African state would be addressed at an appropriate forum. However, the legitimacy of institutions and governments in Africa is a fundamental issue that has plagued the continent since independence.

This chapter examines the legitimacy of political institutions and democratic consolidation in Africa. It argues that the essence of institutions is the legitimacy accorded those institutions. Since legitimacy is so important to the sustainability of institutions, the chapter argues that traditional beliefs, norms, and practices are essential pieces of the institutional puzzle in Africa. This chapter examines traditional societal governing systems that shape political culture and its role in contemporary state institutions. It notes that inherent in traditional institutional system is legitimacy and stability, and that contemporary institutions adapted into Africa's institutional building need to incorporate aspects of traditional institutions.

LEGITIMACY: THE ROLE

Legitimacy creates an environment of acceptance, satisfaction, and, ultimately, stability. Embedded in the concept of legitimacy is the legality of the person, situation, or system. When bestowed on an individual, a sense of joy, belonging, and celebration is the result. When it is bestowed upon a community, its members feel the need to support each other, and loyalty to the community is enhanced. When legitimacy is bestowed upon a system, it is often guarded and protected.[2] In this case we are referring to the legality of the existing system and the rules and processes that created that system.

In politics, the term "legitimacy" connotes the popular acceptance of the system that created the governing authority and/or regime and its laws. When the spirit of nationalism swept through the African continent in the 1950s and 1960s there was the belief that Africa was ready to craft a unique state system, possibly along the lines of the nostalgic African traditional governing systems that had been fundamentally changed and abandoned during the seventy-five years of European colonial administration.[3] However, postindependence African leaders showed no enthusiasm for changing the existing colonial structures and systems.[4]

The change that occurred at independence was basically cosmetic, moving from white-skinned to black-skinned leadership with the new African leaders preoccupied with their personal political survival and the reality of where their respective states ranked in the international arena. Thus any effort at changing the boundaries and domestic institutions would not only be extraordinarily burdensome, but also political suicide for leaders with short-sighted interests in consolidating their rule. Though some African leaders wanted to chart a new ideological space to separate the African people from the colonial past, the fundamental question that may have eluded them in the postcolonial era concerned why the need for change at independence in the first place. Was independence merely the change of the "driver behind the wheel," or the change of the vehicle itself?

There was no question that the legitimacy of the colonial administration and its associated institutions was greatly detested and abhorred, and was the basis for the independence struggle. Senghor,[5] Nkrumah, Kenyatta, Lumumba, and Nyerere denounced racism and systems that were established by the colonial administration and highlighted the illegitimate status of those institutions on the continent of Africa. It was therefore a surprise that none of these leaders truly deconstructed the colonial administrative system, its institutions and structures, in order to construct a legitimate African state. The state system that Africa inherited after independence had no comparison with that of the European nation-states since the African and European experiences were different. Wars constantly shaped and reshaped the boundaries of the European state system and structures.

What is being argued here is not for African states to engage in war to reshape their state boundaries. However, cultural imperatives are essential for state formation. Contemporary conflicts within African states are indications that colonial legacies in Africa, including the nature of state boundaries, is still being rejected. Thus we have seen states split up— South Sudan from Sudan, Eritrea from Ethiopia, Puntland and Somaliland from Somalia, and the nostalgic Biafra state's continual challenge to the Nigerian state.

This discussion goes beyond the issue of discrimination of a certain region or people within the state since not all dissatisfaction toward the government leads to people's calling for secession from the state. The legitimacy of the state as perceived by the people is critical. As mentioned earlier, the current African state reflects an economic imperative of European colonial administration and may have legitimacy challenges. Thus the nature of the African nation-state is at the heart of the issue of the legitimacy of its institutions, politics, and government.

LEGITIMACY: THE CONCEPT

Suchman notes that "legitimacy is a generalized perception that the actions of an entity are desirable, proper, or appropriate within some socially constructed system of norms, values, beliefs, and definitions" (Suchman, 1995, p. 574). This suggests that the value of legitimacy is housed within a given society whose members have a fairly good idea of which institutions and systems are acceptable and deemed appropriate. Legitimacy affects every facet of life in a social space, and when applied to the political environment, its importance is more pronounced.

As Harold Lasswell (2011) bluntly captures in the title of his book, *Politics: Who Gets What, When, How*, Africa's traditional institutions, sometimes expressed in a latent political culture, have overwhelming influence and power over contemporary African institutions and the distribution of resources. The issue of ethnicity that plagues stability in Africa is seen as an African societal challenge. Primordialists have argued that the source of Africa's conflicts is ethnically based. Leaders from particular groups have favored their own ethnic members. Though that may ensure security for the leaders and their governments, this oftentimes leads to marginalization and is not well received by other ethnic groups.

On my research trip to Sierra Leone in 2009, I had the opportunity to interview some members of parliament (MPs) of the opposition Sierra Leone Peoples Party (SLPP). One of the challenges the opposition MPs faced at the time was that the annual devolving fund that the government gives to all MPs to engage in development projects for their constituencies was not ready. Curiously, MPs who belonged to the ruling party at the time had their devolving fund ready and projects were already being undertaken in their constituencies. This may have been exaggerated, but it is not an isolated case. The question of whether or not African leaders are leaders of a particular ethnic group or of all ethnic groups within the state's boundaries becomes critical.

The frequent lack of respect for political leaders and complete rejection of political systems and organizations can be explained by what the

African people deem legitimate regarding institutions and leaders. Africa's political environment, which is characterized by rampant trial and error of regime types, begs the question of whether or not the continent is yet to find the ultimate political order that will pragmatically deal with the broader issues of freedom (a product of the collective nationalistic drive that ushered in independence in several African states in the 1950s and 1960s) and equality,[6] and deemed legitimate within African societies. Nationalism created the state in Africa, but has the state taken care of the nations (i.e., the respective ethnic groups) within its boundaries? Traditional and political institutions and systems have been subjected to the legitimacy test, and where they have failed, chaos has resulted. In Ghana, for instance, first, the lingering chieftaincy conflict in the northern part of the country hinges on who is the legitimate heir to the throne; and second, on the legitimacy of the processes that may have to be put in place in case the two royal houses have to share the throne. These are very complex and challenging situations, but not insurmountable.

In looking at legitimacy from a descriptive lens, Max Weber notes that "the basis of every system of authority, and correspondingly of every kind of willingness to obey, is a *belief*, a belief by virtue of which persons exercising authority are lent prestige" (Weber, 1964, p. 382). Thus the legitimacy of political systems is measured by the confidence and/or acceptance by the people regarding such a system and its leadership. This goes beyond concerns about discrimination, and centers on whether expectations will be met or fulfilled in the foreseeable future by the current institutions and structures. Weber identifies three forms of legitimacy: a system that has been in existence for a long time (traditional), one that the leader has certain attributes that enables him/her to exercise power over the others (charisma), and one that the society has come to accept the legality of the processes that elect people to leadership positions through which those individuals have authority to rule (rational-legal). In Africa, traditional institutions continue to impact and structure society's relations. When people raise questions regarding the confusion brought about by contemporary institutions, they are essentially comparing those institutions to traditional institutions that they deem legitimate.

What is being suggested here is not to abandon modern institutions in favor of traditional institutions. But those contemporary institutions should respond to people's expectation as traditional institutions have done in the past and continue to do.

The chieftaincy institution is one of the formidable institutions in certain parts of Africa. During the colonial era, the colonial administration co-opted some of the chiefs to establish what became known as the "indirect rule." Even in places where chiefs were traditionally nonexistent, positions for chiefs were created. The idea here is that the concept of chieftaincy signifies the presence and continuous impact of the ancestors on the life of the living. The chiefs are expected to play a guardian role by taking care of societal needs, including adjudication of justice, and for the most part, these chiefs have not disappointed. Chiefs have been able to build trust as a result of fulfilling these expectations, and their legitimacy as well as that of the chieftaincy institution has been strengthened. However, chiefs who have abdicated their responsibilities have been dethroned.

Rawls (1993) argued that legitimacy also has normative interpretations in which certain benchmarks are accepted as justified; this could possibly include obligations or responsibility on the part of the political system or the leadership. The normative perception sheds light on the idea that a feedback effect regarding a system's legitimacy includes the system delivering the expected outcomes that the people anticipate. In Ghana for instances there have been numerous instances of chiefs being de-stooled (removing chiefs from office) as a result of nonperformance of responsibility as expected.

Dethronement of chiefs could be done either by the people as in Ghana, or by the state as in Nigeria. In 2013 twelve subchiefs of the New Juaben Traditional Area of Ghana claimed they had dethroned their overlord, Daasebre (Professor) Oti Boateng. They claim to have done this by the invocation of the Otumfuo's Great Oath (Ntam Kesie) after accusing Daasebre Oti Boateng of vindictiveness, dictatorship, and favoritism.[7] In Nigeria, state governments have also been able to dethrone chiefs. In 2005, Alhaji Mustapha Jokolo, the Emir of Gwandu, was dethroned by the Kebbi State government and banished to Gusau in Zamfara State, which is the ancestral home of his mother. He was accused at the time of being an ally of former head of state, Mohammadu Buhari,[8] and also recklessness underserving as an Emir.

Underlying the oftentimes sudden dethronement of chiefs is the issue of legitimacy, which leaves no room for mistakes as a result of the series of oaths sworn during coronation. Thus a dethroned chief may have exhibited behaviors inimical to the health and safety of the society. However contemporary African leaders, though also sworn in by swearing an oath of office, do not want to be "dethroned" or dismissed from office as soon as their government becomes corrupt and misuses public resources. Instead they are quick to urge dissatisfied citizens to vote them out of office if they so wish in the next election. But for now, the citizens should just endure the hardship of elite recklessness that affects the health and stability of the society just as in the case of chiefs.

There is a clear difference between how Africans view their traditional institutions and contemporary democratic institutions. The legitimacy of institutions in Africa underlies their ownership and support. The Nigerian case is a classic one in which political elites could not stand a corrupt chief, but could accommodate a corrupt politician.

The institutionalization of democracy in Africa need not be attached to any foreign assistance. It needs to be structurally developed by the incorporation of traditional beliefs and practices—those that the people understand, own, and will support.

Others have also noted that a system attains legitimacy when it has garnered acquiescence from a majority of people (Raz, 1986). This, however, paves the way for certain types of political authority without their being necessarily legitimate. Military governments in Africa have these characteristics. The populist nature of military governments results from the fact that there happens to be a general perception of a breakdown of the existing system. Expectations are not met, and a sudden intervention is needed right away.

In 2014, the Ghanaian economy was spiraling downward, the currency significantly depreciated against other major world currencies such as the U.S. dollar and the British pound sterling. As a result there were lots of rumors in the country that Ghanaian people would prefer a military takeover to deal with the desperate situation right away. It is to be noted, though, that the military had acquired the legitimacy of creating short-term stability and order within African states. In the long term, military governments are not preferred.

Despite an incredibly perennial challenge against Africa's leadership, the legitimacy of its political systems has not been a focus for discussion. There are both internal and external reasons why this is the case. Internally, it threatens the political survival of elites. Discussions on legitimacy will involve an overwhelming participation of every facet of the population. In the events leading to the end of the apartheid regime in South

Africa, similar discussions went on between the ANC, the National Party, other white right-wing organizations, Inkatha Freedom Party, and Bophuthatswana. It can be costly and raise the issue of whether or not some sections of the society would want to be part of the state. In the case of South Africa, the Afrikaans Resistance Movement (AWB) led by Eugene Terre'Blanche wanted a separate white state.

There seems to be no alternative, however, to Western-style, democratic systems. The bigger question is whether or not, to ensure legitimacy, Western states that have supported African nations in their drive to democracy will be open to alternative political systems that have popular support domestically. Sooner or later, some form of a political democratic system that is not conceptually aligned with a Western concept of democracy may have to be created.

"Democracy" in Africa has morphed into something akin to a patrimonial rule. This is because certain traditional institutional beliefs still wield influence during attempts to establish a democratic system. Patrimonial rules have their own disadvantages apart from their being rejected within international community circles.

The systems bequeathed to African governments by the colonial administration greatly influenced the nature of African political systems. African nationalism was at best an effort to further institutionalize discriminatory colonial structures. Political ideology and systems in Africa were to be judged based on Western-established, democratic systems, which invariably determined the extent to which a state would be accepted and its relationship with the outside world. However, if there is any single discussion so important for postindependence African states, the legitimacy of the domestic political systems should be the priority.

How can African states engage the rest of the world if their internal systems are perceived as illegitimate by their own people? The resulting instability would make any meaningful relationship between Africa and the rest of the world tenuous, as the reality is today. In the immediate aftermath of independence, African leaders became weak domestically due to their failure to respond to needs regarding the existing state institutions. Thus the legitimacy of the state began to unravel.

The so-called Tobar doctrine in Central America was at least an effort to inject legitimacy into political systems and government in Central America.[9] In Africa, when a military leader takes power through a military coup and assassinates a duly elected president, the actions are not deemed murderous or that this military leader has disrupted a stable government elected by the will of the people. In fact, military leaders are hailed as heroes who have come to save the day. There is no accountability, and lots of such individuals, after they are out of office, still want to be appreciated and congratulated for having overthrown the will of the people. Some even come back to announce bids to contest presidential elections, and some actually win elections.

In South Korea, the situation was different. The May 16, 1961, military coup in South Korea that toppled the Second Republic triggered a robust industrialization and economic development in the country and a succession of military regimes for more than three decades. In 1994, Freedom House had a hard time assigning rank to the regime type in South Korea even though the military had engaged in intimidations and human rights abuses. This is as a result of the tremendous economic development achieved under the military rule. The economic development did not hinder the newly elected civilian government from arresting and jailing two former military dictators (Chun Doo-Hwan and Roh Tae Woo) who were part of the military regimes that ruled the country. However, in 1997, President-elect Kim Dae Jung pardoned these former dictators as a sign of reconciliation of the Korean society and state.

In 1963, the first coup in postindependence Africa occurred in Togo and resulted in the death of the Togolese president Sylvanus Olympio. After an initial condemnation and brief ostracism of Togo, probably out of fear that there would be a domino effect in other parts of Africa, Togo was allowed to reestablish relations with other African states and to sign the OAU (Organization of African Unity) Charter, as if this was a good example for others to follow. Military coups continued in several African states afterward.

The legitimacy of the borders of the respective African states is also an issue that needs discussion. The OAU set a minimum standard for legitimacy of African states—that is, whoever controls the capital city basically controls the entire territorial boundary of that particular state (Foltz, 1983, p. 18). This capital city "benchmark," or better still, "doctrine," is problematic, and reinforces the weaknesses in African nation-states. In the contemporary state of Somalia, for example, the government is basically limited to the control of the capital city of Mogadishu and surrounding areas, even with the help of external forces like the United Nations and African Union (AU) forces ready to prop up the "legitimate" government, while its territory contains the two de facto states of Somaliland and Puntland. Many large African states such as Angola and Ethiopia have existed at some point in the post-1950 era as capital-city states.

The classical case of DR Congo is worrisome. Using the capital city benchmark for DR Congo, it follows that whatever entity is in control of Kinshasa (approximately 9,965 sq. km.), an area only a 0.42 percent of the total land area of DR Congo (2,345,409 sq. km), controls the entire country. It is no coincidence that the endemic instability in that country's eastern part consistently plagues neighboring states such as Rwanda, Burundi, and Uganda.

The problem in Somalia has become a serious headache for the Kenyan government to deal with. With a sizable number of ethnic Somalis being Kenyan citizens, the legitimacy of the Somali government and its institutions is unequivocally a priority. This will go a long way to help the Kenyan government in the fight against the extremist group Al-Shabab, which is wreaking havoc in northern Kenya and Nairobi.

A 2015 commitment by the government of Burkina Faso and Niger to redemarcate theirs borders is a step in the right direction. These states have decided to commit to the 2013 ruling of the International Court of Justice regarding their borders. Though the new demarcation will lead to fourteen towns being assigned to Burkina Faso and four to Niger, both former French colonies are satisfied that the huge swathes of land involved will truly ensure the security, peace, and development of both states.

CRISIS OF LEGITIMACY

Legitimacy crises have been present in many societies. However, at the bare minimum, in Africa this has led to political apathy, tensions during elections period, and full-blown conflict in postelection periods. A "legitimacy crisis" is a reduction in the confidence of an institution, leadership, an established system, as well as the functions of those systems (Friedrichs, 1980; Zelditch, 2001; Reus-Smit, 2007). When a legitimacy crisis occurs, the institutions become paralyzed since those institutions then lack the administrative capabilities to achieve any targeted objective (Habermas, 1975).

The United States of America underwent one of the most critical legitimacy crises in the history of an advanced democracy during the 2000 presidential election between George W. Bush, the Republican contender, and Albert (Al) Gore, the Democratic candidate. In the 2000 presidential elections, Al Gore had won the popular vote, but George W. Bush was on the verge of winning the Electoral College vote, the structured and/or legitimized institution that elects the president. What makes this more critical was the fact that George W. Bush's brother, Jeb Bush, was the governor of Florida, the state whose ballots were being contested. The U.S. Supreme Court's intervention and the legal mechanisms that ensued led to George W. Bush's becoming president. This was unprecedented, at least to the generation who watched the whole process unfold. United States citizens have elected their presidents time and again; this time they were denied the opportunity to do so. Many even question the legitimacy of the Supreme Court's intervention to resolve the impasse and influence the election outcome. Some of the questions include: How can unelected officials have a say in who should be the president of the United States? Many at the time perceived the Bush White House as "illegitimate" and serious discussions ensued to scrap the Electoral College system that has elected presidents since long before any living person in America in the year 2000 was born.

The "illegitimacy" of the Bush administration was further exacerbated by America's invasion of Iraq in 2003, and the high financial and human cost associated with the invasion. Though Bush won reelection in 2004, this did not help to divert the critical eye of people ready to critique every policy move he made. In addition, many of George Bush's foreign policies bedevil his younger brother Jeb Bush as he pursues his bid for the 2016 Republican presidential nomination. The point I am making here is that the circumstances leading to George W. Bush's election as president deviated from institutional processes that have sustained the election of U.S. presidents over time, and that left a cloud of illegitimacy in the minds of some people regarding his administration.

The 2006 election in Mexico also provides an example of a legitimacy crisis. Felipe Calderón of the National Action Party (PAN), the winner of that year's presidential election, beat his challenger Andrés Manuel López Obrador. Though not quite unusual for a candidate leading in the earlier opinion polls to lose the elections, the circumstances that surrounded the administration of the voting process defied what was believed to be acceptable by the voting public (at least supporters of Obrador). The company that was awarded the contract to design the electronic computing system for counting the votes, Hildebrando Corporation, had Calderón's brother-in-law and Calderón's sister as senior partners. In that year's elections Calderón recorded 35.89 percent of the votes, and Obrador had 35.31 percent, making it a difference of 0.58 percent of votes between them.[10] Just as in the U.S. case, Mexico also faced a crisis of the legitimacy of the president himself and that of the electoral institution. In both cases, unusual events that may be coincidental threatened the existence of long-established electoral processes and institutions.

In 2008, president Robert Mugabe was faced with a legitimacy crisis after the elections that year. Mugabe has won successive elections by fair or foul means since 1980 when Zimbabwe attained its independence. However the 2008 election became a pivotal moment in his political career when suddenly he was faced with a legitimacy crisis as a result of most members of SADC (Southern African Development Community, an inter-governmental organization made up of countries in southern Africa and headquartered in Gaborone, Botswana) criticizing him. African countries and the international community refused to endorse his presidency after emerging victorious from the June 27 runoff election. His challenger, Morgan Tsvangirai of the MDC (Movement for Democratic Change, a political party in Zimbabwe), withdrew from the runoff citing intimidation and intense violence in the country. The Zimbabwean Electoral Commission ignored these concerns, went ahead to organize the runoff election, and declared Mugabe as president.

As the United Nations condemned the polls, observer missions from the AU, SADC, and the Pan-African Parliament noted that the election was not in line with regional and international standards. Though African leaders acknowledged that Mugabe was legally in power after he was inaugurated on June 29, 2008, he lacked both legal and political legitimacy. Neighboring Zambia and Botswana, key allies to Zimbabwe, criticized the outcome of the election. Also at the AU Summit, Nigerian Foreign Minister Ojo Maduekwe noted that his country did not recognize Mugabe's legitimacy.[11] It was also noted that Thabo Mbeki, the then South African president and who was seen as a longtime ally to Mugabe, had told Japanese Prime Minister Yasuo Fukuda at the G8 Summit that year that there was no legitimate government in Zimbabwe. Mbeki suggested to Fukuda that there was a need to form a unity government. Other African leaders such as Omar Bongo of Gabon, Pakalitha Mosisili of Lesotho, and the Mozambican government offered support for Mugabe.

The pressure that was mounted on Mugabe led to the creation of a unity government in Zimbabwe for the first time, with Morgan Tsvangirai as the prime minister and Mugabe, the president. The five years of power sharing were the most tumultuous the country has ever seen until it was ended by the 2013 election when Mugabe won, and the prime minister's position was officially abolished.

What happened to make Mugabe feel the intense pressure regarding the legitimacy of his rule? After all, he had won elections since 1980. For the first time, Zimbabweans came close to experiencing what they had long expected—that a free and fair election, which is a characteristic of democracy, could actually be achieved in Zimbabwe. With the economy ailing since 2000, the suppressed voices of the electorate could then be heard.

IN SEARCH OF A POLITICAL ORDER

Explanations for causes of conflicts and instability in Africa are varied. Causes of conflict in African societies have ranged from weaker political systems and institutions to issues of economic marginalization. As policy makers, researchers, and the global community seek ways to address domestic insecurities within African communities, which also has consequences for the global security, attention has largely been focused on the adaption of Western-style democratic political order. Though this system has some benefits (as it largely broadens the base of political participation and grants political power to the people), its adoption in Africa as a form of political system has not achieved the intended goal of truly empowering the average citizen as it has in Western, advanced states. Within African societies, political elites have largely used the democratic process to instead make citizens politically weakened.

Stability has been the bedrock for development. Democratic systems have ensured political stability in Western societies. However, democracy has not resulted in anticipated stability within African societies. Actors interested in which political system works within particular societies have failed to recognize that the issue of legitimacy underlies political systems. As discussed, though legitimacy involves beliefs and perceptions, expectation is a key factor in legitimacy. Thus political legitimacy derives its strength—its power—from whether or not the people are satisfied with the type of political system they have and the extent to which such a system delivers expectations.

The history of a political system is the history of the legitimacy of that system. Since legitimacy has to do with people's perceptions and beliefs, it is also dynamic. France's political history records the power of the monarchy that ruled the country for a long time. However, at some a point the French people determined that the monarchy was no longer legitimate and did not meet the expectations of the people. The political history of the United States also followed the same trend with the Declaration of Independence in 1776, which enabled the citizens of the former British colony to chart a new political system in line with their new culture and expectations. Africa, however, seems to be at a crossroad regarding which political system is compatible with its cultures and historical experiences, and which will create a stable society, fulfill expectations, and deliver development.

Since culture and experiences have a role to play in legitimizing systems, African traditional institutions and the colonial experience are relevant to Africa's search for a viable political system. How did African societies govern themselves before the colonial experience? To what extent are colonial institutions either compatible or incompatible with African cultures? These issues have not been seriously addressed in Africa's quest for institutional development and stable political systems. Political systems not only establish relationships between leaders and the people, but also commitment to each other.

Political order has always been contrasted to anarchy. Thomas Hobbes ([1668] 1996, p. 84) in his book *Leviathan* describes life in the state of nature as being "solitary, poor, nasty, brutish, and short"; to ensure order, survival, and stability within societies, Hobbes advocates a social contract in which the people within a society submit their rights and liberties to a "sovereign" or a "stronger individual" in exchange for protection. The idea here is that as power becomes concentrated and preponderant in the hands of an individual (or a government) it will create an environment where the notorious bully will be frightened to indulge in arbitrary harassment, order is restored in the society, and everyone lives peacefully. Again, the assumption here is that the "strong individual" would act as an enlightened dictator and take care of the weak or at least create an environment for the weak to survive.

African societies in the past have organized themselves mainly through giving legitimacy to leaders to establish rules with regard to establishing relationships between individuals in the group. The close contacts that people in these communities have between them legitimized the predominantly patrimonially controlled societal order. Modern political order since Westphalia has changed the way organized groups within a particular geographical region should view each other and the extent to which the power of the state dominates the power of traditional societies. Colonial and postcolonial African societies became entrapped in a political order of having to submit individual liberty to an "imaginary government" that is remote and that makes the rules and supposedly ensures security and a stable political order. Again the complexity of the situation could also be seen within the reality that Africa, at the dawn of independence, had no choice (at least from what African leaders viewed at independence) regarding which political system to adopt. The temptation to catch up with the rest of the world was so intense that the continent literally had to adopt state and political systems practiced by advanced democracies with different cultures and societies.

Consistent with the above observation is the dominant theory that describes how newly independent states could quickly integrate into contemporary Western political systems in order for them to modernize and catch up quickly with world development. Modernization theorists[12] have argued that in political terms, "institutional expansion, the rationalization of governmental apparatus, power concentration, some measure of political participation and an augmentation of capacities in order to meet growing demands" (Chazan et al., 1992, p.15) are essential in a country's bid to modernize. Thus modernization was seen as providing newly independent African states the foundation upon which to realize some form of political stability and autonomy, and also to mimic, and probably be like, the Western industrialized world. Though these institutions of governmental capacities could achieve the results predicted, proponents of the modernization school failed, in their model, to account for how such governmental institutions and capabilities came to be or developed in the first place in the Western world. Also they failed to recognize the impact that fragmented African societies could have on these institutions and how capable African societies are to embrace this phenomenon.

Comparative political scientists such as Guy Peters (1998) have emphasized the need to consider cultural relativism, since different meanings and explanations are accorded concepts across systems. Did African states make the right choice by adopting foreign political systems at their time of independence? Could African states, and for that matter, African societies, have taken the time to craft appropriate political systems consistent with their social realities? Does the Western political order obstruct Africa's efforts in this direction? Have African countries found appropriate political systems? If they have, why do domestic instabilities abound in many African states?

Political instabilities in Africa raise the question of whether African states have found appropriate political order. In other words, the issue of what political system can ensure sustainable government in Africa has become a critical debate in finding solutions to conflictual societies in Africa. Understanding Africa's traditional past and institutions of government could assist in this discourse since the prospect of according legitimacy to institutions is enhanced.

Some research on the onset of civil conflict has indicated that ethnic heterogeneity has a negative impact on state stability. (This is the primordialist line of argument.) Evidence also shows that civil conflicts clearly arise between identifiable groups in Africa. In Ghana for instance, the recurring conflict in the northern part of the country has made the military base in the north of Ghana the most strategic endeavor ever to be embarked upon by the Ghanaian government The civil war between the Hutus and the Tutsis and the subsequent genocide in Rwanda and Burundi in 1994 and the ethnic and nationality conflicts in Nigeria and Liberia are examples. The democratization process that is supposed to help societies with ethnical tensions to overcome those tensions has not delivered on those expectations. Thus the legitimacy of the democratization process and democracy as practiced in Africa is seriously in doubt.

Campaigns and election periods have now become the most dangerous periods that ordinary Africans have to deal with. In addition, it has become the norm for parties that lose elections to reject the election result. The violence that ensued after the 2007 elections in Kenya and the 2008 elections in Zimbabwe are just two examples of not accepting the legitimacy of democracy or its process in Africa. There have also been widespread allegations of vote rigging during elections, and certain African leaders with no term limits win elections time and again. This has had negative effects on democratic consolidation.

To what extent could traditional African institutions, derived from Africa's cultural experience, assist in shaping a viable political order in Africa?

TRADITIONAL AFRICAN SOCIETIES

The organizational structure in traditional societies is unique and clearly defines roles. In traditional societies "the bonds of kinship provide the primary basis of political and economic activity" (Palmer, 1989, p. 53). It is observed that each family, and for that matter the extended family, acts as an independent political actor on its own. In some cases this relationship could extend to the coming together of clans and tribes that seek to ensure greater security. Traditional societies develop close-knit structures in which individual roles are clearly defined, as are rewards and punishments for behaviors.[13] In some cases stronger tribes absorb weaker ones in the process; however security and basic human needs are provided. For instance, the Ashanti kingdom in Ghana, which started as a family, has grown powerful enough to absorb other Akan tribes and even some tribes in the northern part of Ghana, and has been able to manage these societies with fewer conflicts.

The uniqueness of these types of systems is that though leaders are accorded sacred status, they discharge their responsibilities toward the people as they would for the revered ancestors. There is a clear understanding of what the role of the people is as well as the role of the leaders. The relationship between the leaders and the governed is not different from the relationship that (should) exist between the leadership and the citizens in contemporary democracy as practiced in Africa. Western democracies elect representatives from constituencies. These representatives represent their respective constituencies in government. Thus African states should be able to incorporate traditional beliefs and organizations into contemporary representative government without much problem. How can African societies transfer the close-knit bond between leaders and subjects to that of a bond between representatives and constituents? How can the relationship that existed between diverse ethnicities in Africa be coalesced in order to establish a strong relationship between representatives and constituents?

TRADITIONAL INSTITUTIONS, LEGITIMACY,
AND AFRICA'S NATION-STATES

Having discussed the importance of traditional beliefs and institutions in African societies, examining governmental capacities become a priority. Obviously, the discussion so far does not support the thesis that African states, by virtue of the nature of its diverse society, are inherently unstable. Beliefs, relationships, mutual performance of responsibilities, and fulfilled expectations are critical factors that ensure stability within those societies.

In developing an appropriate political order to achieve a more stable and sustainable state, the expansion of governmental capacities is critical. The priority is to bring together those who wield power and their subjects so they are as close as possible. An expansion of governmental capabilities needs to align governmental institutions with the socioeconomic needs of the subjects (Chazan et al., 1992). This is essential since in African traditional societies, leaders have taken care of societal needs, including providing justice, and subjects have also responded appropriately. Contemporary African leaders need to go beyond petty ethnic cleavages since the democratic process they have embraced requires such an attitude. Establishing institutional legitimacy in Africa is a challenging task; however, there is no room for hypocritical attitudes. Establishing institutions and providing the expected outcomes are the bases for institutional legitimacy.

Strong governments are essential for political order. What does strong government mean in the context of African societies? Does it mean that the military should be in control of government and point guns at the heads of citizens to force the setting aside of differences so as to achieve the ultimate goal of order and stability? Or does it mean, as Hobbes (1668) noted, there will be the need for a dictator, who somehow is stronger than everyone else, to govern with a strong arm in order to redirect the people's attitude from cultural differences to the goal of nation building? The role of the military in nation building has been mixed. The modern military has the capability of restoring short-term stability (Halpern, 1962). The military could serve as a guarantee to discourage chaos that could inhibit development (Bell, 1965). Does this mean that civilian governments in Africa should hand over power to the military when there is a sudden disturbance that has the potential to cause instability? Would not the military try to take advantage of the situation and usurp power only to turn around and rationalize their acts by arguing that time is up for a short intervention? Human rights, sustained stability, and development under military governments in Ghana, Nigeria, Gambia, Sierra Leone, and Liberia have not been encouraging.

Other scholars have also suggested that by working closely with the bureaucracy, the military's role in politics and development is enhanced (Horowitz, 1966). Would the military be able to work with bureaucrats when the civilian government they overthrow could not do the same? However, Halpern (1963) is quick to note that only political parties have the ability to instill a sense of citizenship and public participation in political decisions.

The international community has not been friendly to military governments. Some have put enormous pressure on military governments to reverse course in states such as Mali and the Central African Republic. Canada for instance threatened to withhold aid to Mali when the military took over in 2014. This led the coup leaders to hand over power. After the military took over power in 2014 when the president, Blaise Compaore, fled the country, the international community put a lot of pressure on the Burkinabe military to make them establish an interim government right away to guide the nation back to democracy. Non-governmental organizations (NGOs), international financial institutions, and civil society organizations have also exerted pressure.

Is multipartyism and democracy the way forward for African states in their quest for political order and nation building? How can multiparty democracy transcend strong ethnic cleavages in order to mobilize the people for nation building and stability? Can multiparty democracy play the role of traditional societies by being able to anticipate and meet the varied needs of the diverse ethnicities? The reality is that African states have less choice when it comes to the form of government they can craft. The stage has already been set and the way to go, so far as the type of political system is concerned in this contemporary world system, is multiparty democracy.

There are several advantages that show the wisdom in this form of government. First, societies elect representatives who represent them in parliament and pass legislation that enhances constituents' welfare (all things being equal). Should the elected officials fail to deliver what is expected of them, they would be voted out in the next election.

However, most of these public officials go down to the nation's capital and forget to discharge the responsibility for which they were elected. Simply voting them out of office has not been an effective punishment due to the perennial nature of the problem. Elected officials continue to be out of touch with their respective constituencies and the state itself continue to lack development. Elected office tenures range between four to five years, by which time the elected officials have probably accumulated enough properties to live on their own when voted out of office. Weak institutions that promote corruption and lack of accountability result from such behaviors. Weak institutions benefit the rational calculation of elected officials. Organizing elections at short intervals could help stem the situation, and a recall rule could be put in place if the leader loses legitimacy among the constituents.

Multiparty democracy, which provides an opportunity for diversity and expression of preferences in government, is definitely the way forward. However, when the unique characteristics of African societies are considered, adapted forms of democracy could be developed to suit the African setting.

This chapter has discussed negotiating the issue of legitimacy in Africa's quest for a sustainable political order. The chapter notes that African traditional societies are embedded with characteristics that could embrace modern liberal democratic models. However what is important is the ability of government to create institutions that foster opportunities so people have confidence in the system. Thus this chapter considers the issue of legitimacy as critical for institutional building and democratic consolidation in Africa. Single party systems, military regimes, and even democracies in Africa have been challenged by issues of legitimacy. Thus analyzing the essence of legitimacy is critical to the way forward as Africa tries to embrace a democracy that is functional and that could lead to the building of viable institutions.

NOTES

1. "Legitimacy" comes from the Latin verb "legitimare," meaning lawful.

2. As in many states, past experiences and political culture influence their constitutions and laws.

3. For readings on African traditional ruling systems, see G. Ayittey, "The Native System of Government: A Summary and an Assessment," in *Indigenous African Institutions*, 2nd ed. (New York: Transnational Publishers, 2006), pp. 265–310; and J. F. Bay-

art, "Introduction: The Historicity of the African State," in *The State in Africa: The Politics of the Belly* (London: Longman. 1993).

4. For more readings on the challenges of establishing a legitimate and sustainable African state, see J. Herbst, "The Political Kingdoms in Independent Africa," in *States and Power in Africa: Comparative Lessons in Authority and Control* (Princeton, NJ: Princeton University Press, 2000), pp. 97–113; B. Davidson, "The Black Man's Burden," in *The Black Man's Burden: Africa and the Curse of the Nation State* (New York: Times Books, 1992), pp. 197–243; and Crawford Young, "The Heritage of Colonialism" in John W. Harbeson and Donald Rothchild, eds., *Africa in World Politics: Reforming Political Order*. Boulder, CO: Westview Press.

5. This is Senghor's discussion on Negritude. Negritude is an ideology and literal philosophy expressed among francophone intellectuals against France's racism in its colonies. It encouraged common black racial identity to combat French racism.

6. Nationalism created the state in Africa, but has the state taken care of the nations within the respective boundaries in African states?

7. Otumfuo is the head of the Ashanti Kingdom in Ghana. It is believed that the people of New Juaben owe allegiance to the Otumfuo. Thus, by invoking the Great Oath of the Otumfuo, the twelve chiefs showed the legitimacy of their claim to dethrone the Overlord of New Juaben, Daasebre Oti Boateng.

8. Buhari is currently the president of the state of Nigeria.

9. In March 1907, the then foreign minister of Ecuador, Tobar, declared that the signatures of five Central American states would be needed to recognize any government that came to power through coup d'état or revolution. It was incorporated into two agreements in 1907 and 1923. After El Salvador and Costa Rica pulled out, the United States and other Western states have favored the Estrada Doctrine, which views this agreement as offensive to the sovereignty of other states, and that government recognition should be based on its de facto existence rather than its legitimacy.

10. See Alejandro Álvarez Béjar, "Mexico after the Elections: The Crisis of Legitimacy and the Exhaustion of Predatory Liberalism," *Monthly Review—An Independent Socialist Magazine* 59 (3, July–August 2007), http://monthlyreview.org/2007/07/01/mexico-after-the-elections-the-crisis-of-legitimacy-the-exhaustion-of-predatory-neoliberalism/ .

11. Ojo Maduekwe was Nigeria's foreign minister from July 2006 to March 2010.

12. See Samuel Huntington, "The Change to Change: Modernization, Development, and Politics." *Comparative Politics* 3 (3, 1971) pp. 55–79; and Irene Gendzier, *Managing Political Change: Social Scientist and the Third World* (Boulder, CO: Westview Press, 1985).

13. For more information, see Monte Palmer, *Dilemmas of Political Development: An Introduction to the Politics of the Developing Areas* (Itasca, IL: F. E. Peacock Publishers, 1989).

SIX

Democracy and the Politics of Petroleum

Comparative African Perspectives

Ali A. Mazrui

This chapter discusses democracy and the politics of petroleum.[1] It examines the dynamics of natural resources and democratic consolidation. A fundamental argument made is that the discovery of petroleum and other mineral resources before democracy poses a major challenge to the democratic process and democratic consolidation.

The discourse regarding the nexus between resources, security, and stability in the developing world is well documented.[2] However, not much has been explored to put this reality within a theoretical perspective to enable this relationship to be studied in terms of Africa's democratic experimentation and consolidation. Resources, as a factor of production, have been a key element in the development expeditions of states (of both developed and emerging economies).[3] From an institutional point of view, proper regulation and management of natural resources has a positive effect on development and stability as management of these resources takes into consideration the nature of the society, people's expectations, competition, and equity.

One of the missions of the African Union Peace and Security Council is the African Union Border Program (AUBP). With the focus on African integration, borders of respective African states are now reconceptualized as bridges to facilitate movement of people and goods from one country to the other. As a result, resources such as land, water, and wildlife, which often pose potential conflict situations to people living along border towns, can safely be shared without any conflict occurring. There have been improved cooperation at the interstate and local levels in border towns between countries such Zambia, Malawi, and Mozambique in southern Africa, and between Mali and Senegal, and Mali and Burkina Faso in West Africa. The reality is that people living in border towns are more interested in the ease with which they can relate and the lasting relationships that result from such relationships that includes trade, family, and security. The issue of which nationality one belongs to is secondary to the essential goal of forging those relationships. Thus, AUBP is facilitating this reality through increased cooperation between neighboring states in order to ensure peace, security, and development.

Within states in Africa petroleum resources have a tremendous impact on the nature of the society. The challenges and dilemmas of petroleum resources to the respective oil-rich countries can also be seen with respect to the prospect for sustainable democratic transitions and consolidation. Managing petroleum resources sometimes becomes intractable with some even describing it as a "curse." On the economic side, it is clear that, for lack of any cheaper source of energy, petroleum products will continue to be relevant in global economic discourse, and as such every state that possesses that resource is definitely bound to be wealthy and witness improvement in its economy. On the other hand, petroleum resources have been a challenge to democratic consolidation. It has stifled opposition to government hold on power, and political elites have tried as much as possible to reduce the democratic space, including democratic engagement with the people. The end result has been insecurity within those states. I will discuss this issue within the context of the paradox of Nigeria and Libya's abundant oil resources, the volatility of petroleum resources in those states, and the challenges that volatility poses to democratic consolidation.

I happen to regard the politics of petroleum as a much bigger issue than whether Nigerian oil is domestically subsidized or not. There are huge issues connected with petroleum as Nigeria's premier natural resource. I regard the issue of oil-subsidies as relatively minor when compared with the impact of petroabundance on the divide between the rich and the poor in Nigeria and between industry and agriculture, and upon the struggle to democratize Nigeria.

Does a resource-rich African country find it easier or more difficult to stabilize democracy? Nigeria has of course been an oil-rich country throughout its life as an independent country. Has Nigeria's oil wealth helped or hindered its efforts at democratization and democratic consolidation?

This chapter argues that if natural resources are discovered after democracy has started maturing, the new wealth will help stabilize the democracy. But if the mineral wealth comes before democratization, it could delay the democratizing process.

A positive example outside Africa is the discovery of oil resources in the waters of Norway and Scotland. This was a case of economic enrichment of already mature democracies. In the case of Norway, the oil has strengthened the welfare state and stabilized democratic governance. This is so because democratic institutions ascribe political power to the people. Thus, political elites face the prospect of rewards and punishment regarding how they manage the economy, including natural resources.

In the case of Scotland, petroleum initially deepened Scottish nationalism and heightened separatist sentiment for a while. But the longer-term consequences have given Scotland a regional legislature and more solid influence within the United Kingdom. The arrival of economic enrichment after substantial democratization has stabilized the democratic order in both Norway and Scotland. Obviously the support of the people is critical to make a strong case for control of natural resources. Consequently it becomes difficult for elites to disregard the needs of the people when the control of natural resources is secured.

With a developing country like Nigeria, on the other hand, petrowealth preceded stable democratization. The country became independent with three huge provinces forming a federation that was inherently unsustainable for long. The oil wealth was mainly in the Eastern region. The debatable point was whether the petrowealth contributed to the level of self-confidence of Eastern Nigeria. Did this trigger the Eastern-led, military coup of January 1966? Did the East seek to more effectively control the petroleum located in their own region? And when Eastern Nigerians later became victims of the Northern countercoup and the genocidal anti-Igbo massacres, did the petroleum in the East strengthen the late Chukwuemeka Odumegwu Ojukwu's resolve to attempt secession from Nigeria? Predemocratic petrowealth had created impediments to Nigeria's democratic progress—a major institutional challenge.

Another African example of the development of natural wealth before national democratization is the former Belgian Congo, upon attaining independence in 1960. Eastern Congo at the time was almost as well-endowed as Eastern Nigeria—but the Congo had Katanga minerals rather than petroleum. Just as oil wealth later triggered separation and attempted secession in Eastern Nigeria, copper and other mineral wealth inspired Moise Tshombe to attempt the secession of Katanga from the former Belgian Congo. In the second half of the twentieth century, both Nigeria and Congo Kinshasa illustrated the proposition that natural resources before the stabilization of democracy was likely to negatively impact further democratization.

On the other hand, the Republic of South Africa had selective democracy for white people a century and a half before extending the full franchise to black people and other South Africans of color. Whites had relatively free and fair elections for themselves, but not for the rest of the population. The country had a working parliamentary system, and a judiciary that had relative independence within the constraints of a racial political order. Even at the height of apartheid, South Africa was acquiring democratically relevant experience.

Did the fact that South Africa had a racially selective democracy, alongside prior mineral wealth, help postapartheid South Africa to enhance its democratic order? The relevance of institutions cannot be overemphasized. Postapartheid South Africa, sans discriminatory apartheid institutions, no doubt did inherit strong state institutions bequeathed to it by the apartheid era. Though allegations of corruption and inefficiency have been leveled against some political elites, there is no reason to believe that South Africa will fall into some form of authoritarian or military regime. South Africans know too well that total rejection of oppression and discrimination were the goals that drove the fight against the apartheid regime. South Africa has enormous mineral wealth, and any additional mineral exploration will only strengthen democratic institutions and state-citizen relations (rather than harm that relationship).

While the Congo had seen its democracy collapse within a year of attaining independence, and Nigeria had a military coup within less than six years of attaining sovereign status, since 1994 and the end of apartheid, South Africa continues to have the most liberal constitution in Africa's entire history.

Postapartheid South Africa not only extended the franchise to citizens of color, but also abolished the death penalty, enhanced freedom of the press, freely elected three different presidents since 1994 (Presidents Nelson Mandela, Thabo Mbeki, and Jacob Zuma), recognized gay rights, and legalized same-sex marriage and civil unions. Even selective democracy, combined with simultaneous mineral wealth, provided subsequent opportunities for further democratization.

However, all three well-endowed countries (Nigeria, the Democratic Republic of the Congo, and the Republic of South Africa) had to confront a shared threat to democracy—the threat of plutocracy, a society ruled by a very small number of wealthy people. The effect is the total disregard of social responsibility. Substantial mineral and petrowealth in these three countries created a potential rivalry between rule by the wealthy and rule by the people. Let us turn to these dilemmas more fully.

DEMOCRACY VERSUS PLUTOCRACY?

Oil-rich Third World or developing countries are indeed caught between the reality of plutocracy (rule by the rich) and the aspiration toward democracy (rule by the people). The wealth of petroleum creates great disparities in income and major differences in economic power. On the other hand, the population as a whole can become restless for a greater say in how the wealth of the nation is distributed.

In addition to the choice between plutocracy (the power of wealth) and democracy (the power of votes), Nigeria was for a while disrupted by militocracy—the power of soldiers and the military. Indeed, during much of the second half of the twentieth century, Nigeria was controlled more by soldiers than by either the economically rich or by people's power. Nevertheless, the country's petrowealth created additional motivation for the military to control the economy.

Here it is worth distinguishing between *coup-prone* African countries like the Congo (Kinshasa) and Nigeria from the mid-1960s to the end of the twentieth century, and *coup-proof* African states that have never experienced military governments since independence. *Coup-proof* African states include South Africa, Senegal, Tanzania, Zambia, Kenya, Zimbabwe, as well as the Kingdom of Morocco.

Ghana also used to be coup-prone. In this twenty-first century, Ghana has become less coup-prone by demonstrating how an incumbent ruling party can be outvoted and be peacefully replaced. When such a change occurs through the ballot box more than once (as it has in Ghana), the prospects of becoming a coup-proof country improve. Since Ghana started producing oil in 2010, the oil revenue has not impacted the country's economic outlook positively, at least from the point of view of reducing the level of poverty. However, there is no reason to believe that oil exports will reverse Ghana's democracy and its consolidation in the foreseeable future.

The twenty-first century seems to have made Nigeria and the Congo less and less coup-prone, but unfortunately, more and more conflict-prone. The Niger Delta has been repeatedly disrupted by conflict and terrorism. Sabotage to the oil resource itself also occurs. And the tensions between Christians and Muslims have often exploded into violence—including terrorism against such totally innocent foreigners as United Nations personnel. In the former Belgian Congo a succession of civil wars has killed millions of Congolese.

In addition to plutocracy, democracy, and militocracy, Nigeria has been struggling with meritocracy (rule by the learned and the skilled). Independent Nigeria's first head of state was Nnamdi Azikiwe (popularly known as Zik). Azikiwe was not a philosopher-king, but he was arguably a philosopher-president. I met Zik at Lincoln University in Pennsylvania where I was one of the speakers in his honor in the last quarter of the twentieth century. His particular leadership in Nigeria's early years was interpreted as a sign that Nigeria would develop into a meritocratic system of government—with leadership coming disproportionately from the educated class. This was in contrast to the Congo, which in 1960 had only a handful of college graduates. Unfortunately the military coup in Lagos in January 1966 interrupted the merit-symphony in Nigeria. Instead a whole generation of militocracy was inaugurated.

Ironically, the Nigerian civil war (1967–1970) reactivated elements of meritocracy within the separatist Eastern Region (Biafra). The Igbo had revealed technological skills in the second half of the twentieth century. Indeed, their triumphant economic skills in Northern Nigeria in the 1950s and 1960s contributed to their vulnerability as a people in 1966. For a while Eastern Nigeria was well endowed in education as well as in petroleum. The East was both skill intensive and resource intensive.

During the Nigerian Civil War innovativeness among the Igbo produced Africa's first-locally made gun vehicles. During that Biafran conflict, the Igbo displayed levels of innovation that were unprecedented in postcolonial African history. The Igbo created rough-and-ready armed militarized vehicles as well as the beginnings of Africa's industrial revolution. This renaissance was aborted by the oil bonanza from 1997 onward.

Although warfare is inherently destructive, it also often releases inventiveness. During the Biafra War, Nigeria was more internally innovative than externally prosperous. The Nigerian Civil War produced some of the high points of Nigeria's experience with technological innovation. Meritocracy manifested itself. However, the Nigerian oil bonanza after the 1973 OPEC (Organization of Petroleum Exporting Countries) price escalation created disincentives to Nigerian enterprise.

War had indeed brought out both the best and the worst of Nigeria in human terms. But *technologically* the power of spilled blood in Nigeria produced greater innovation than the power of spouting petroleum. The pain of Biafra was technologically more fruitful than the profit of OPEC. However, democracy continued to be elusive in the last quarter of the twentieth century.

ON THE SHORES OF TRIPOLI

A fourth resource-rich country that has been instructive is Libya under the late Muammar Gaddafi. Libya was oil-rich long before it could even experiment with democratization. Gaddafi was definitely not ideologically a "democrat," but he did have some egalitarian tendencies. As a de facto head of state, he declined such ostentatious titles as "President" and "His Excellency." His Green Book was not a manual for democracy, but it was a manual for a more participatory society and a more inclusive world system.

Gaddafi used his petrowealth partly to assert that a small country can be a player on the world stage, and not merely a pawn in the hands of the big powers. Over the decades Gaddafi was involved in such international conflicts as supporting the Irish Republican Army, funding the Palestinians, financing Muslim rebels in the Philippines, subsidizing Louis Farrakhan of the Nation of Islam in America, and trying to defend Idi Amin from both his domestic and international adversaries.

Gaddafi also increasingly used his petrowealth in support of Pan-Africanism and the solidarity of African states. He helped finance some of the liberation movements in southern Africa before the collapse of apartheid. He subsidized some of the meetings of the Organization of African Unity (OAU) and some of the projects of Afro-Arab solidarity under UNESCO in Paris, France.

Gaddafi also allowed citizens of some neighboring sub-Saharan African countries to find varied kinds of jobs in Libya. He invested in development projects in such countries as Mali, Niger, and even Kenya. Gaddafi's Libya owned multiple hotels in other African countries.

With Libya, as with Nigeria and the Congo, resource wealth before democratization was an impediment to genuine maturation of democracy. But Gaddafi did try to promote a more egalitarian society, a more inclusive global system, and African solidarity.

On the whole Gaddafi in the last two or three decades in office had been a good African, but a bad Libyan. He had been a bad Libyan by being intolerant of dissent and being too long in power. Although he rejected titles like President or His Excellency, and preferred to live in a tent, he did suppress critics uncompromisingly.

But if he was a bad Libyan, in what sense was he a good African? He invested in African countries often at great loss and on limited returns for himself. He financed expensive African conferences from his own resources. He supported the very expensive Arabic translation of the eight-volume UNESCO *General History of Africa*.

Black Africans had jobs in Libya when they were rejected elsewhere. Many young Malians who enlisted to go to fight for Gaddafi in 2011 did so out of sentimental attachment to the Libyan leader. Black faces fighting for Gaddafi were not necessarily mercenaries. Gaddafi's money could have bought better-skilled mercenaries than the peasants of Mali and Burkina Faso. East European mercenaries would have been better trained.

Over dinner in Gaddafi's tent as his guest some years ago, I found myself defending the Arabs against Gaddafi's hostility. I was also astonished when Gaddafi asked me to send him a copy of my father's book, *The History of the Mazru'i Dynasty of Mombasa*. It was part of Gaddafi's fascination with Afrabia. The book was published by Oxford University Press in the 1990s.

By early January 2011 Gaddafi had paid a price for preferring his African identity. He had alienated fellow Arabs to a disastrous extent. The Arab League virtually gave the green light to the Security Council and the Western powers to bomb Gaddafi's Libya. His fellow Arabs threw him under the bus!

On the other hand, Gaddafi's Libyan adversaries in Benghazi had been stimulated by the prodemocracy uprisings in Tunisia and Egypt.[4] Petrowealth had not prepared Libyans for democracy, but the fall of Hosni Mubarak opened up new democratic possibilities for a while, with Mohamed Morsi's short-lived election as president of Egypt. What Libya's oil could not achieve, Libyan revolutionaries tried to accomplish with the help of the North Atlantic Treaty Organization (NATO) and American air power.

It is not clear how far Gaddafi allowed himself to be constrained by Islamic law both as a leader and as treasurer of his country's wealth. He might have found a way of paying *zakat* (Islamic tax). But he was certainly unsure whether Islamic banking, with its distrust of interest, was appropriate for the billions of petrodollars generated by Libya's oil industry.

How much of the petroleum of both Africa and the Middle East comes from countries that are subject to Sharia? The biggest Sharia producers of petroleum are of course Saudi Arabia, Iran, Kuwait, and the United Arab Emirates. Their national systems of law are partly informed by Islamic law.

There are other oil producers that are selectively subject to Sharia either in chosen portions of law (such as personal law) or chosen provinces of the country (such as the Sharia states of Nigeria). Such partial Sharia oil producers also include Iraq, Bahrain, Algeria, and the contested area bordering the Sudan and the Republic of South Sudan.

It used to be said in the twentieth century, "Where there was sand, and there were Muslims, there might be oil." This coincidence was because the deserts of the Middle East had yielded billions of gallons of petroleum. But although Nigeria has the largest concentration of Muslims on the African continent, Nigerian oil is not located primarily in Muslim areas. Similarly the oil in the two Sudans may indeed coincide with a lot of sand, but not necessarily with a lot of Muslims. In the old Sudan a combination of the Sharia in the north and the discovery of oil in the south crystallized separatist demands from the south. In Nigeria the concentration of both petrowealth and political power in the south helped to trigger Islamic nationalism in the north. Aspects of Shariacracy illustrated what was exceptional about Nigeria while other aspects of the Sharia manifested what was typical of postcolonial Africa as a whole (see tables 6.1 and 6.2).

THE GENDER QUESTION IN OIL-RICH AFRICA

The issue of gender to some extent measures the level of democracy and its consolidation within societies.

Let us return to the late Gaddafi before he was lynched by his own people. Muammar Gaddafi had ruled Libya since the military coup of 1969. He had been less important as a social or religious reformer domestically than in his efforts to be a political player globally. How far did Islam affect his attitude toward women and the gender question?

On the gender question Gaddafi used symbolism. Far from regarding women as unsuited for military roles, or incapable of using firearms efficiently, Gaddafi theoretically entrusted his life to female bodyguards. These were often referred to as "the Amazons." Women in oil-rich Libya were more liberated than in oil-rich Saudi Arabia. Was Gaddafi influ-

Table 6.1. Shariacracy Between Typicality and Exceptionalism

Typicality	Exceptionalism
Nigeria inherited a legal system based primarily on British law, but with minor amendments to suit local conditions in each colony. Typical of other colonies.	Nigeria is the only African country outside Arab Africa which has seriously debated an alternative to the western constitutional and legal option.
Both constitutional arrangements and criminal law were primarily based on western systems of order.	That is what the debate about the *Sharia* is partly about.
The language of interpreting the constitution and interpreting the laws was the imperial language, English.	Exceptionalism includes the fact that Nigeria is the largest concentration of Muslims on the African continent.
In Nigeria, as in most former colonies, this imperial and legal order was seriously flawed and did not deliver constitutional stability or respect for the law. Whither Rule of Law?	Exceptionalism therefore includes the fact that Nigeria has more Muslims than any *Arab* country, including Egypt. But can exceptionalism support *Sharia* at the State level combined with secularism at the federal level?

Table 6.2.   Between Lingo-Constitutionalism and Religio-Constitutionalism

Typicality	Exceptionalism
Whether a federal system should permit cultural self-determination for its constituent parts has been faced by other federations before.	Initially Nigeria's federation allowed cultural self-determination for neither language nor religion.
Switzerland concedes cultural self-determination but in terms of language but not religion. Some cantons are officially French-speaking, some German-speaking, and some Italian-speaking.	What the Sharia debate has opened up is whether religion, rather than language, should be the basis of the cultural self-determination for constituent units in Nigeria.
India concedes cultural self-determination in terms of language—different states have a lot of say on the official language of the state.	In Quebec, English-speaking Canadians have no choice but to put up with Francophone state schools and Francophone road signs.
Canada is coming to terms with a Quebec that insists on making French the sole language of Quebec. The English-speaking minority in Quebec is disadvantaged.	In Zanfara should non-Muslim Nigerians similarly have to accept their minority status and conform? Or is that undemocratic?
	Is an imposed lingo-cultural policy any different from an imposed religio-cultural policy for the relevant minorities?

enced by the memory of the widow of the prophet Muhammad Aisha? Riding in the middle of the battle, she participated in the Battle of the Camel during the Caliphate rivalry.

The Pope in history has had the physical protection of the Swiss guards and the spiritual protection of the Virgin Mary. Gaddafi had women bodyguards who were spiritually required to be virgins. On the link between virginity and military effectiveness, Gaddafi in North Africa in the twenty-first century had shared a characteristic with Shaka Zulu of South Africa in the eighteenth century. Zulu wanted his male soldiers to be celibate, totally denying themselves sex. Gaddafi had wanted his female guards as virgins from the start—and committed to celibacy until military retirement.

But since the Libyan war erupted in February 2011, there has been no evidence of female soldiers fighting to protect Gaddafi. Actually, there have been more female warriors in the opposition in Benghazi than among Gaddafi's forces in Tripoli.

Much more interesting was Gaddafi's decision from the 1990s that he was an African first and an Arab second. Having first begun as a Pan-Arabist, he got disenchanted with fellow Arabs. His gender policy was perhaps more African than Arab. And in his last twenty years in office, he had put his money more in Pan-African ventures than in Pan-Arabist projects. He saw himself less and less as heir to Gamal Abdel Nasser of Egypt and more and more as heir to Kwame Nkrumah of Ghana. His foreign policy was less informed by Islam than by anti-imperialism. His colorful dress culture was more reminiscent of West Africa than of the Arabian Peninsula.

Let us now look at the gender question more broadly in postcolonial Africa. Uganda had gold mines before it prospected for oil. Did this affect gender issues?

Uganda has had a woman for vice president under Yoweri Museveni (on and off) since the 1990s, but Uganda had a woman foreign minister as far back as the regime of Idi Amin in the 1970s. Both Liberia and Kenya have repeatedly had women presidential candidates who campaigned hard for the ultimate political office. Ellen Johnson Sirleaf in Liberia did lose to Charles Taylor and Charity Ngilu in Kenya did lose to Daniel Arap Moi, but both women put up a spirited fight and demonstrated substantial support. Since then Ellen Johnson Sirleaf has served as the first elected woman president in Africa's history. She has shared the Nobel Peace Prize 2011 with two other women (Leymah Gbowee of Liberia and Tawakkul Karman of Yemen).

In the 1980s Winnie Mandela was the most famous African woman in the world. She was of course a South African. Mrs. Albertina Sisulu is another high-ranking South African woman. Frene Ginwala served as speaker of the postapartheid parliament in the Republic of South Africa before the United States had a female Speaker of the House, Nancy Pelosi.

Before Rwanda and Burundi collapsed in the 1990s they were experimenting with women prime ministers. Unfortunately Rwanda soon exploded into interethnic genocide as the year 1994 recorded the fastest genocide (an estimated 800,000 people (mainly Tutsis) lost their lives in 100 days) in the history of the world.

For quite a while Nigeria was at the level of having its highest-ranking woman as a minister for women's affairs. Nigeria has since moved up to have full cabinet level female ministers and a couple of other ministers of state. Female empowerment has since included a brilliant woman minister of the economy Ngozi Okonjo-Iweala. This may be significantly better than a number of other African countries. Female Nigerian talent has included reciprocal transfer between the Nigerian government and the World Bank in Washington, D.C.; Ngozi Okonjo-Iweala has served both as director of the World Bank and Nigeria's finance minister.

In addition, Nigerian women are among the most economically independent in the whole of Africa. They are assertive individuals, and many of them know how to play the market. In some cities a female plutocracy is in the making.

Nigerian women in scholarship and science compare well to Nigerian men, and female academic leaders have become widespread. It is true that Liberia had a woman president of a university long before Nigeria had a woman vice-chancellor, but as a country Liberia has since been led by a woman Nobel Laureate. And now Nigeria is catching up—first with a woman vice-chancellor at the University of Benin, and later with another female chief executive at the University of Abuja. Lagos State also started early with female academic leadership. Nigerian educational institutions are in dire financial straits, but within these constraints there is optimism that Nigerian women professors will not be left too far behind Nigerian men in the arts and, hopefully, in the sciences and engineering.

Nigerian women were not in high-profile positions during the era of *militocracy*, when the country was coup-prone and repeatedly dominated by soldiers in power. These were the years from the mid-1960s to the end of the twentieth century. The country's petrowealth also laid the foundations of a *plutocracy*. Nigerian women participated in the plutocratic bonanza, but far behind Nigerian male beneficiaries.

Women as voters were slow to wield their influence, especially in Northern Nigeria. However, women as parliamentarians have increased in the twenty-first century, and some have served as cabinet ministers in the executive branch. A woman head of state in Nigeria was inconceivable during the era of militocracy, but before the middle of this twenty-first century, a female president in Nigeria is conceivable as part of democratization. What Liberia has achieved may be repeated by a Nigerian woman in the years ahead.

Oil wealth had been an impediment to democratization in the first fifty years of Nigeria's independence. As this twenty-first century unfolds further, will the empowerment of women be the vanguard of wide democratic change? Will petrowealth at last be the mother of government by the people rather than government by the affluent?

Nigeria has experienced a rich systemic diversification since independence. The country has experimented with federalism, militarism, liberal democracy, meritocracy, and Islamic law (the Sharia). But the country still needs an architecture of governance that is solidly institutionalized.

While predemocratic petrowealth slows down democratization, it does produce opportunities for a welfare state. Gaddafi's Libya was a kind of welfare state—affording medical, educational, residential, and other forms of subsidies to the citizens.

Nigeria's petrowealth did not result in a welfare state to serve all Nigerians but resulted in a local oil market that was subsidized. In addition, on many occasions poor Nigerians helped themselves to oil outside the constraints of the law.

An oil-rich, developing country faces the dilemma of choosing between using the national resources to create a welfare state or allowing its citizens to have subsidized access to the commodity without a welfare state. In the case of Nigeria, subsidized oil and cheaper petroleum reduced the cost of energy locally, but without a national health service or subsidized housing. Gaddafi's Libya, on the other hand, had provided elaborate welfare services without necessarily subsidizing the local energy market.

Subsidizing petroleum does promote cheaper electricity and helps those who own cars. But such subsidies are more elitist and more selective than is a full-scale welfare state. Abundant oil wealth may not necessarily help political democratization, but it can enhance economic rights and promote welfare opportunities for the citizenry.

In the case of Nigeria subsidized energy was one of the benefits of petrowealth. While in the first fifty years of independence Nigeria was very coup-prone, the new political horizons have reduced the frequency of military rule but have aggravated conflict situations. Both Nigeria and Congo (Kinshasa) have become less coup-prone, but unfortunately remain highly vulnerable to conflicts.

To conclude, I have attempted to illustrate how resource richness before democratization reduces the motivation for democratic reforms. Wealth that is not created but only produces an affluent *elite of leisure* rather than an *elite of labor*. The system that emerges is closer to a *plutocracy* rather than *democracy*. We have used examples from two oil-producing countries (Nigeria and Libya) and two resource-rich, but not oil-based, economies (South Africa and the Democratic Republic of the Congo). Other countries have also been mentioned to sharpen points of comparison and contrast.

The struggle for democracy and the struggle for peace have become conjoined. It is still an open question when the abundant resources of each country become a force for stability rather than a trigger for discord.

NOTES

1. This chapter adds to earlier works on Nigeria by the author (Ali A. Mazrui) including *A Tale of Two Africans: Nigeria and South Africa as Contrasting Visions,* ed. James N. Karioki (London: Adonis and Abbey Publishers, 2006).

2. See Paul Richards, *Fighting in the Rain Forest: War, Youth and Resources in Sierra Leone* (Oxford: James Currey, 1996).

3. Natural resources could include mineral deposits such as gold, diamond, uranium; crude oil and natural gas; fresh water bodies; beaches; the rain forest, and the like.

4. Mostly referred to as "Arab Spring," this was a revolutionary wave of change for democracy and equity in the Arab world that began in Tunisia in December 2010 and involved other nations such as Egypt, Libya, Yemen, Bahrain, and Syria.

SEVEN

Uhuru Bado Kidogo

Africa's Condition of "Not Yet Uhuru"

Ali A. Mazrui

This chapter discusses the challenges to consolidated political and societal freedoms in Africa. The title "Uhuru Bad Kidogo" joins *Uhuru*, which means "freedom or independence" in Swahili, and *bado kidogo*, which means "not quite yet achieved" in Swahili. Though I chronicle these challenges through the life of Jaramogi Oginda Odinga, the core argument focuses on historical and cultural values and institutions that need to be incorporated regarding Africa's quest at accomplishing sustainable political freedom.

Two assassinations in Kenya in the 1960s had significant consequences for Jaramogi Oginga Odinga. One was the assassination of Pio Gama Pinto,[1] a Kenyan born Asian, who had three political passions—serving Africa, serving socialism, and helping Jaramogi Oginga Odinga. When Pinto was killed in 1965, Oginga lost a gifted political organizer, as well as a friend. But Pinto did not produce a heroic successor after his martyrdom.

The second assassination of the 1960s, which shook Oginga Odinga's career, was the murder of Tom Mboya in 1969.[2] Mboya was Odinga's ethnic compatriot and political rival.[3] His death unleashed riots and demonstrations among the Luo and led to Oginga Odinga's detention and the banning of his political party. But the Mboya assassination did not lead to a Mboya political successor either, whereas Odinga's natural death did result in at least one high-profile, political Odinga after him.

Oginga Odinga's obstacle toward the presidency was persistently ethnic. There was a concerted effort to prevent a Luo from becoming president. In comparison, John F. Kennedy's primary obstacle toward the presidency was religious. The United States had never had a Roman Catholic president. John F. Kennedy faced the challenge of whether, when the chips were down, he would be more a follower of the Vatican than of American democratic values. He had to convince the American public that he was more American than Catholic.[4] Both Oginga Odinga and Raila Odinga have tried their utmost to convince Kenyans that, when the chips were down, the Odingas were Kenyans first and Luo second.

But, has the Kenya electorate regarded the Odingas in the reverse order—as Luos first and Kenyans second? When Oginga Odinga argued that *Uhuru* had not yet been achieved, and offered to lead Kenyans toward social justice, he looked to see who was following him. It was not underprivileged Kenyans regardless of ethnic background. It was fellow Luo, regardless of income or social class.

As far as the Kenya electorate was concerned, the messenger was more politically relevant than the message. The message was a call for greater social justice, but the messenger was judged by his ethnicity. That was one major reason why *Uhuru* was in a state of *bado kidogo*. Oginga Odinga's concept of "not yet Uhuru " signified a freedom gap caused by the forces that inhibited internal democracy and curtailed external sovereignty. This gap may be a systemic or institutional reality that hinders democratic consolidation in Kenya's society.

TOWARD CLOSING THE UHURU GAP

There were seven strategies for narrowing the freedom gap and realizing full Uhuru. Within each of these strategies across time, Oginga Odinga played a historic role.

The most vital for the people is *the strategy of democratization*—the belief in freedom through democratic process. Oginga Odinga was elected to the Kenya colonial legislature in the year and month when the Gold Coast in West Africa became independent—March 1957 (Atieno-Odhiambo, 1997, pp. 8–10). But, unlike the Gold Coast (later Ghana), Kenya had an entrenched white settler presence. Oginga Odinga joined forces with Tom Mboya in the struggle against white settlers' privileges and for the release of the imprisoned national leader, Jomo Kenyatta (Atieno-Odhiambo, 1997, pp. 12–13).

A more dramatic blow for democracy struck by Oginga Odinga occurred when he was invited to the residence of the governor, Sir Patrick Renison, and offered the leadership of the first African government in colonial Kenya. This event occurred in Government House (now called State House) in Nairobi in 1960. The British governor and the Kenyan nationalist were both standing when the offer was made. It seemed to be the chance of a lifetime. It turned out to be Oginga Odinga's last opportunity to become premier of Kenya on the eve of independence. Oginga Odinga is reported to have responded as follows to the governor: "If I accept your offer, I will be seen as a traitor to my people. The British cannot elect me leader to my people . . . . Kenyatta is around, just here at Lodwar. Release him and allow him to lead us; he is already our choice" (Oruka, 1992, p. 6).

Sir Patrick Renison was temporarily stunned. He then summoned the driver to take Mr. Oginga Odinga back to his native quarters in Nairobi.

We now know that Oginga Odinga had struck a blow against external selection of African leaders. He had sacrificed what turned out to be his last opportunity to lead Kenya. His incumbency could have transformed the ethnic configurations of postcolonial Kenya. If Oginga Odinga had accepted the governor's offer, the Jaramogi could have presided over the release of Jomo Kenyatta, and Kenyatta might have become Odinga's vice president instead of the other way round.

If Odinga's first blow in favor of democracy was to reject external selection of African leaders, Odinga's second blow in favor of democracy was to challenge the doctrine of one-party monopoly of power. The Kenya African National Union (KANU) and the Kenya African Democratic Union (KADU) had merged to form a one-party system. Oginga had prospered under KANU first as vice president of the party, then as minister for home affairs (1963–1964) and then as vice president of Kenya and minister without portfolio (1965–1966) (Atieno-Odhiambo, 1997, p. 21).

Yet he broke away from KANU and formed the left-of-center Kenya People's Union (KPU). He gave Kenya a two-party system based on an ideological divide (left versus right) rather than the original two-party system based on an ethnic divide (KANU under big tribe leadership and KADU under small tribe alliance) (Atieno-Odhiambo, 1997, p. 23).

But in 1969 KPU was outlawed and Oginga Odinga was detained for a while. He rejoined KANU upon his release in 1971, but the Kenyatta regime prevented him from running for political office. After Kenyatta died in 1978, the succeeding regime under Daniel Arap Moi continued to prevent Jaramogi Oginga Odinga from challenging the power monopoly of the KANU establishment (Atieno-Odhiambo, 1997, p. 25–27).

In 1992, I (Professor Ali A. Mazrui) held a press conference in Nairobi at which I called upon President Daniel Arap Moi to step down from power. I argued that President Moi had outlasted his welcome in the political process. Never until then had a Kenyan citizen openly called for the resignation of an incumbent president at a press conference within Kenya itself.

My remarks caused an uproar in the country. What I was not expecting was a request from Jaramogi Oginga Odinga to meet with me at my hotel, the Intercontinental in Nairobi. From my point of view, there was a serious risk that our meeting would be regarded as an apparent political alliance. Nevertheless, I decided to meet publicly with Oginga Odinga at the Intercontinental for coffee. It was a moment of solidarity rather than the forging of an alliance. He and I agreed that President Moi had been in power too long. What we did not realize in 1992 was that Moi was going to remain in power for another ten years.

However, something positive occurred in the course of Daniel Arap Moi's final decade as head of state. At long last, the country reopened itself for multiparty politics—a system that Oginga Odinga had attempted to initiate when he created the left-wing Kenya People's Union party in the mid-1960s. He later fought for multipartyism through the Forum for the Restoration of Democracy (FORD) (Atieno-Odhiambo, 1997, pp. 31–32).

Ironically, Oginga Odinga was a great fan of Kwame Nkrumah, the man who virtually invented the African one-party state. Nkrumah had argued late in the 1950s that Ghana was too dangerously divided to risk a multiparty system. Julius K. Nyerere argued a few years later that Tanzania was too solidly united to afford the luxury of a multiparty system. Jaramogi Oginga Odinga admired both Nkrumah and Nyerere. In fact, after Nkrumah's death in 1972, Odinga described Nyerere as "the Nkrumah of today" (Oruka, 1992, p. 56).

Yet both presidents were architects of the African one-party state—an experiment that widened the freedom gap in postcolonial Africa. At a prodemocracy meeting held in Nairobi in 1993, I argued that Kwame Nkrumah had dealt a blow against open society in Ghana, partly by inventing the one-party state and partly by attempting to destroy the independence of the judiciary in Ghana. My old paradoxical conclusion was that Kwame Nkrumah was a great African, but not a great Ghanaian.

To my surprise, Oginga Odinga reacted very strongly to my criticism of Kwame Nkrumah. He even suggested that I had been unduly influenced by foreign critics of African heroes. The passion of Odinga's reaction was particularly surprising since this was a meeting to celebrate the emergence of legal opposition parties in the final decade of the twentieth century.

In the 1960s Odinga had rebelled against the one-party state and formed his own opposition party (the KPU). In the early 1990s Odinga was heading another opposition movement (FORD) against KANU and against Moi's leadership. Yet Oginga Odinga leaped to the defense of his old hero, Kwame Nkrumah, in spite of his being the inventor of the African one-party state. Odinga reacted passionately to my criticism of Nkrumah.

By the time the twenty-first century opened, Raila Odinga, Jaramogi's son, had emerged as an opposition leader, sometimes consolidating his own party, and sometimes operating within a ruling coalition. The debate had shifted from the old issue of whether the country could afford a second political party to the new issue of whether the country should have a prime minister with independent powers. Would the Uhuru Gap be narrowed if there were better checks and balances? Could an independent prime minister help provide some balance to the powers of the presidency? The democratization process is still unfolding in postcolonial Kenya—even when two steps forward are followed by one step backward.

TOWARD INDIGENIZING FREEDOM

The second major strategy for narrowing the Uhuru Gap is the process of indigenization. This involves tapping indigenous values, traditional technologies, native cultures and languages, and ancient paradigms.

Kenya's struggle for Uhuru was well above average in utilizing indigenous culture as part of the military engagement. That was what the Mau Mau war was all about. The liberation fighters in the forests had their own elaborate oaths of allegiance, taken by naked men, in ceremonies that involved the skin of a sacrificed goat.[5]

The old Dar es Salaam school of African historiography in the 1960s distinguished between primary African resistance to colonization and secondary African resistance. The primary resistance was supposed to have occurred in the initial years of colonization when the Europeans were coming in and the Africans were trying to stop them. The Maji Maji war in Tanganyika against the Germans early in the twentieth century was a case of primary resistance.[6]

On the other hand, the anticolonial struggle by the Tanganyika African National Union (TANU) against British rule in 1950s was secondary resistance. The nationalists were themselves Westernized or semi-Westernized, and were using some of the cultural values of the British to fight the British. Slogans like "self-determination" and "democracy" were being thrown at bewildered British colonial officials left, right, and center.

Dar es Salaam historians like Terence Ranger have interpreted the concepts of "primary resistance" and "secondary resistance" chronologically. The primary phase occurred earlier in African history (like the Maji Maji war in 1905–1907), while the secondary phase involved Westernized Africans later in history.[7]

What the Mau Mau fighters illustrated was a different sense of "primary resistance." In the case of Mau Mau, the term "primary" was cultural rather than chronological. In the 1950s in Tanzania, TANU was fighting the British in a nonviolent secondary resistance chronologically during the same period Mau Mau were fighting the British in a primary resistance culturally. In this cultural sense, the term "primary" refers to the use of indigenous paradigms, native symbols of warriorhood, and even indigenous weapons like the spear and the panga.

Of all the liberation movements of Africa in the twentieth century, Mau Mau was the most indigenously inspired, indigenously authentic, and even indigenously led by leaders like Dedan Kimathi. Mau Mau also constituted the writing on the wall for the British Empire in Africa. Mau Mau speeded up the liberation not just of Kenya, but also of Tanganyika, Uganda, Zanzibar, Somaliland, Zambia, and Malawi. The British, however, interpreted Mau Mau as a compelling sign that it was time to close the entire chapter of colonialism in Eastern Africa.[8]

But, simultaneously with Mau Mau, Kenya's struggle for independence also included secondary resistance by nationalists like Tom Mboya and Oginga Odinga. Yet much more than Tom Mboya, Oginga Odinga was sensitive to the need for indigenous symbolism.

During India's struggle for independence, the British had to get used to Mahatma Gandhi's modest attire—the *dhoti*. Winston Churchill called Gandhi "the naked fakir," but Gandhi persevered in the symbolism of what he wore.[9] In the words of Shakespeare's Polonius, "For the apparel proclaims the man."[10]

Oginga Odinga's apparel proclaimed him when in 1958 he entered the Legislative Council in Nairobi wearing African attire, complete with sandals (*akala*). And for much of the rest of his political life, Jaramogi Oginga Odinga wore an African cap of beads.[11]

The strategy of indigenization in Kenya also required a choice of language policy. On this issue Oginga Odinga was less historically relevant than Jomo Kenyatta. Kenyatta's command of the Swahili language was almost the equivalent of a native speaker. Kenyatta's Swahili oratory was much more impressive than the Odinga's.

Partly because the first president of Kenya was comfortable with the Swahili language, Kenyatta was an important champion of Kiswahili as a national medium of communication. For a brief period Kenyatta even compelled the Kenyan Parliament to adopt Kiswahili as the main language of parliamentary debate. All of a sudden the great English language orators of yesterday became mediocre speakers of Kiswahili—while the modest English speakers of yesterday rapidly rose to towering Swahili eloquence the day after.

In Kenyatta's final years of life he gave Kiswahili a parliamentary opportunity while his own life lasted. There were indeed contradictions in the policy. Speeches in Parliament were made in Kiswahili, but much of the Hansard, the record of the parliamentary debates, was still in English. The language of politics in Kenya was more than ever Kiswahili, but the language of the Constitution of Kenya was still defiantly English. Budgets were presented in Parliament in the English language, but debated in the House in Kiswahili.[12]

Perhaps President Daniel Arap Moi's compromise after Kenyatta's death in 1978 made the best sense under the circumstances of Kenya. The Kenyan legislature would be deemed to be bilingual—allowing members to speak in either English or Kiswahili, while addressing the rest of the country more in Kiswahili than in English.

While in linguistic terms Jomo Kenyatta was a figure of more cultural authenticity than Jaramogi Oginga Odinga, in family terms Kenya's Luo leaders were better rooted in indigenous traditions. While Kenyatta was partly socialized by the Christian missionaries, Jaramogi Oginga Odinga was especially cultivated by Luo elders.

There was also the tradition of levirate in Luo culture.[13] When a husband dies, a Luo widow, was not cremated live as in Hindu tradition. The Luo widow was remarried to a relative of her late husband, either a brother or a cousin. The children of the deceased husband became the children of the new husband.

Oginga Odinga's mother became a widow quite young. She was then remarried to a cousin. The second husband was called Odinga. It is a name that has now been immortalized in Kenya's history. When Tom Mboya was assassinated in 1969, his widow, Pamela, was remarried to Tom Mboya's brother. The ancient Old Testament tradition of the levirate was alive and well in indigenous Luo culture.

As we have mentioned earlier, one of Oginga Odinga's heroes was Kwame Nkrumah of Ghana. Nkrumah's father also died when he was very young. His mother was inherited by, or remarried to, one of his father's siblings. Nkrumah's second father was a product of the levirate tradition in African indigenous culture.

The culture of Hinduism had argued that the widow of a deceased man reconciled herself to her loss by being burnt with her husband. African culture had a different argument. The widow of a deceased man reconciled herself to her loss by being married to a relative of her deceased husband.

Perhaps even more long-lasting as a strategy of indigenization is the gradual re-traditionalization of Africa's educational concepts and curricula. Western-style schools have been the disproportionate instruments of the education of African children in the postcolonial era. How indigenously African is the curriculum? How indigenized is the study of history, literature, philosophy, and general education? The entire African educational system is crying out for a truly indigenizing cultural and pedagogic revolution.[14] The use of indigenous language in debating day-to-day issues that affect society is critical. We sometime wonder whether elites such as legislators understand each other when debating essential business that affects the development of the state when they use a foreign language.

TOWARD AFRICANIZING THE AFRICAN STATE

The third major strategy of closing the Uhuru Gap is the strategy of domestication. This involves making foreign institutions in Africa more relevant to Africa's needs or more compatible with African cultures and traditions. Such foreign institutions sometimes need to be domesticated in the sense in which a wild beast might be subjected to domestication.

The most important foreign institution in colonial Africa has been the actual state itself—with all the paraphernalia of flags, national anthems, regular embassies abroad, a special foreign ministry at home, and relative compliance with international law. The modern state also has a standing army, and sometimes a navy and an air force.

Before European colonization there were city-states like Zanzibar and Kano and old-style empire states in Africa such as the Songhay, Mali, and Ghana empires—and also the Ethiopian imperial state for hundreds of years. Egypt has also been a state of some kind across thousands of years. Intermediate traditional states included Bunyoro-Kitara and Buganda.

What were missing were modern-style nation-states with modern concepts of sovereignty and national integration. In any case, much of the rest of Africa was stateless. Some African societies were even examples of ordered anarchy—such as the precolonial Somali people.

European colonization has bequeathed to Africa over fifty states with artificial borders and with systems of government that were alien to African traditions and culture. How was Africa going to "domesticate" this wild beast called the modern state?

One element in the strategy of state domestication was to try to get a constitution that was as rooted as possible in African traditions of governance and African political values. In the initial struggle between the Kenya African National Union (KANU) and the Kenya African Democratic Union (KADU), it was in fact the minority party, KADU that held the most promise of being close to African traditions and values. KADU originated as a federation of the Kalenjin Political Alliance, the Maasai United Front, the Kenya African People's Party, the Coast African Political Union, and the Somali National Association (Ogot and Ochieng', 1995, p. 65).

KADU wanted a constitution that was based on a federal recognition of ethnic diversity in the country (Ogot and Ochieng', 1995, p. 70).

KANU's stand was a quest for national homogeneity and more centralized government. KANU was also gradually leaning toward a quest for the one-party state. The KANU agenda seemed more compatible with modern concepts of the state, but somewhat distant from African traditions of decentralized governance. The KANU agenda was not trying to recapture the precolonial Kenyan legacy of *weak governments and strong traditions*. Unlike West Africa and Ethiopia, Kenya never had empire-states. Yet, KANU was aiming for the level of centralized government in Kenya that was almost internally imperial.

Oginga Odinga, in the early 1960s, belonged to the KANU frame of reference. He regarded the KADU agenda as "tribalist" and the KANU program as "nationalist." The Kenya constitution that finally emerged for the early phase of independence was the *majimbo*[15] constitution, which did aspire to turning Kenya into a federation of cultures. Oginga Odinga complained that the document was convoluted, too long, and potentially divisive. But the majimbo constitution was closer to respecting indigenous traditions of governance than were the republican changes that were made by KANU in 1964–1965, and the subsequent centralizing and tightening of governance in 1982 (Ogot and Ochieng, 1995, p. 94).

If domestication of the state was one of the requirements for closing the Uhuru Gap, the abandonment of the spirit of majimbo was a blow against the Africanization of the state. Oginga Odinga came to realize in subsequent years that marginalizing the Kalenjin, the Coastal people, the Maasai, and the Somali could one day lead to the marginalization of the Luo by a Kikuya-dominated government. And when the Kalenjin got the upper hand from 1978 to the end of the twentieth century, even the preponderant Kikuyu tasted what it was like to be marginalized.

The majority of postcolonial states in Africa convinced themselves that they were ready-made nation-states, and they opted for unitary systems of government. But unitarism was often incompatible with Africa's own indigenous legacies of weak governments and strong traditions. Apart from Nigeria, the word "federation" as an internal constitutional system became a dirty word in most African countries.[16] And yet the unitary state has been a disaster in one African country after another—partly because unitarism was a break from precolonial African styles of governance. Even Nigeria has failed as a federation partly because it has combined formal federalism with militarized unitarism throughout most of its postcolonial history. [17]

Oginga Odinga interpreted Luo culture as a paradigm that "did not have a central government with somebody at the top of it who would be accountable to the whole community." [18] And, yet, Oginga Odinga opposed the decentralizing concept *majimbo*. Kenya's original federalist constitution envisaged a two-chamber legislature and six constituent regions whose powers were derived from the constitution and not from the central government The six regions were to have their own legislatures, "state-governments," and jurisdiction over land issues and the police. Particularly impressive for an African constitution were the procedures for changing the constitution. The procedures, though less stringent than those of the United States, required 75 percent majority in the lower house and a 90 percent majority in the Senate before the constitution could be amended. [19]

Oginga Odinga complained that these were checks without balances. "The new constitution would start Kenya's government off under severe handicaps" (Odinga, 1967, p. 230). Oginga Odinga lived to appreciate the need to make constitutional amendments difficult rather than easy. In his interviews with the late Professor H. Odera Oruka, in the 1990s, Oginga Odinga complained as follows:

> Some leaders are fearful and untruthful in their dealings with the people. They initiate policies and go on to implement them without bothering to consult the people. The Kenya of the First Republic provides examples of this. . . . Take also the example of the decision to make Kenya a one-party state [in law] in 1982. It was announced one morning in Parliament that within two or three days, Kenya was to be a one-party state. (Oruka, 1992, p. 101)

In the course of his postcolonial career, Oginga Odinga moved from a distrust of checks and balances to a greater appreciation of their value. This faith in checks and balances has been carried further by his son, Raila Odinga. In the Raila Odinga paradigm, checks and balances are needed not just between the executive, the legislature, and the judiciary, but also within the executive branch itself. Raila Oginga and his supporters have pushed for an office of prime minister, independent of the presidency, [20] and yet in coordination with the head of state. Oginga Odinga had once complained about *majimbo* as "checks without balances." Raila Odinga seeks the establishment of a prime minister more as balance with the presidency than as a check against the presidency. Traditional African philosophy is more comfortable with the concept of parallel balancing of the power of the chief than countering or checking it.

The new proposed Boma Constitution of Kenya echoes aspects of the legacy of majimbo of forty years earlier.[21] Greater recognition of regional autonomy and of ethnic diversity is part of the process of re-Africanizing the African state. They also help in narrowing the Uhuru Gap in the postcolonial era.

DIVERSIFICATION: DOMESTIC, INTERNATIONAL, AND CROSS-CULTURAL

The fourth strategy of narrowing the freedom gap is the strategy of diversification. Areas that needed to be diversified include crops grown in Africa, trading partners, foreign aid donors, and Africa's external role models. In addition, a better balance between agriculture and mineral resources is needed.

It was certainly not adequate to look at only Western civilization for paradigms of change and progress. Oginga Odinga led the way in postcolonial Kenya by daring to look beyond Western Europe and the United States for donors, potential trading partners, and paradigms of development. In the heat of the Cold War, Oginga Odinga was the most daring of all Kenyans by being willing to explore what the Communist world had to offer to help Africa. Liberation fighters in southern Africa looked increasingly to Communist countries in both Europe and Asia for arms and military training. Oginga Odinga believed that the Communist world could also lend a hand in economic development and social transformation. In that spirit of learning from others, Oginga Odinga came to say the following in retrospect in the 1990s:

> I traveled to [the then] Soviet Union, to China, and several Eastern European countries. . . . Having been schooled in the capitalist-dominated world, it was natural to feel that. . . I should visit other sections . . . . I was an inquisitive visitor, but I did not become their religious disciple—I did not become a communist. (Oruka, 1992, p. 87)

A number of times in the 1950s and 1960s Oginga cultivated and befriended a number of leaders in Communist countries. And, just as liberation fighters in southern Africa received weapons and training from Communist countries, Oginga Odinga and his movement received economic and financial support from the Soviet Union, Eastern Europe, and China. Tom Mboya, on the other hand, received support from Western Europe and the United States.[22] Kenya experienced the diversification of benefactors in the Cold War era.

In 1960, Tom Mboya succeeded in providing an American airlift to enable Kenyan students to study in the United States.[23] Oginga Odinga managed to balance that with scholarships for Kenyan students to study in the Eastern bloc. Raila Odinga studied in Communist East Germany. Such international balancing helped to narrow the Uhuru Gap.

Tom Mboya had cultivated links between the trade unions of Kenya and those of the Western world. Oginga Odinga successfully helped to establish the Lumumba Institute on Thika Road to train activists and leftist youth wingers. Kenyatta himself opened the institute on Jamhuri Day in December 1964. While Western resources subsidized Western-style organizations in Kenya, Oginga Odinga negotiated different forms of foreign assistance from different socialist countries. Cinema vans were received from Czechoslovakia, lecturers came from the Soviet Union, books and blankets from Yugoslavia, financial support from the German Democratic Republic (East Germany) and from the People's Republic of China. [24]

Oginga Odinga insisted that he was a socialist and not a communist. Just because he had friendly relations with Communist countries did not make him a communist. Later on, he gave the following illustration:

> Take the example of former U.S. President Richard Nixon. Nixon was the first U.S. president to visit Mao Tsetung's China; that was in the early 1970s. Nixon broke through the ideological iron curtain between communist China and the U.S.A. . . . . They ate together with Mao Tsetung and Chou En Lai . . . . Did President Nixon and Henry Kissinger become communists? . . . What I did by visiting China and the Soviet Union was no more than Nixon did. (Oruka, 1992, pp. 87–88)

In apparently backing the Soviet Union, Oginga Odinga had backed a loser. The Soviet Union had collapsed by the time Odinga died in 1994. On the other hand, by backing the People's Republic of China, Oginga Odinga was backing a future winner. We know today that China is on its way up the ladder in the struggle for world supremacy and toward becoming the next superpower.

One real friend of the socialist world was Oginga Odinga, who belonged to the world of the imagination, while Double-O (Oginda Odinga) belonged to the real world of thought and action. Perhaps this is a distinct area of diversification: a combination of thought, action, and the imagination.

No less illustrative of thought, action, and the imagination is the world of religion. Like his hero, Kwame Nkrumah, Oginga Odinga was an ecumenicalist. Odinga regarded religion as both a basis of diversity and a foundation of human oneness. He said, "I do not differentiate between the various denominations. I see religion qua religion as being something that is needed to help people inculcate discipline in themselves. On the face of it, most religions preach the brotherhood of man to man" (Oruka, 1992, pp. 38–39).

Kwame Nkrumah went further in his view of the role of religion in Africa. It was in his book *Consciencism* that Nkrumah most explicitly addressed the triple heritage of African culture, Islam, and what he called "Euro-Christianity." For Nkrumah, the biggest challenge for African philosophy was how to synthesize these three very different traditions of thought. Nkrumah's concept of "consciencism" was the nearest approximation of my own concept of the "Triple Heritage"—a search for an African synthesis of three distinct civilizations.[25] Nkrumah felt that Africa needed what he called

> the theoretical basis for an ideology whose aim shall be to contain the African experience of Islamic and Euro-Christian presence, as well as the experience of African traditional society and, by gestation, employ them for the harmonious growth and development of that society . . . .
> Our society is not the old society, but a new society enlarged by Islamic and Euro-Christian influences. (Nkrumah, 1964, pp. 68–70)

Nkrumah described this "consciencism" as a "philosophy and ideology for decolonization" in his book (Nkrumah, 1964), the synthesis of the three civilizations was a quest to narrow, if not fill, the Uhuru Gap.

The implementation of such cultural synthesis would require major changes in Africa's educational systems. Most African schools and universities started off as primarily Western-style institutions. The postcolonial period has seen some progress in "domesticating" educational systems and syllabi by covering more African history, literature, philosophy, and culture. But the teaching of African languages is still grossly neglected in most African countries.[26]

And, if Africa is a continent of three civilizations (indigenous, Islamic, and Western), when will African schools and universities pay enough attention to Islamic history, philosophy, and literature, or the culture and politics of the Muslim world?

A diversification of the syllabus and the curriculum, even beyond the triple heritage is what Africa needs. The West, Islam, and our own ancestors are not the only sources of wisdom. Africans can learn a lot from the cultures and experiences of India, China, Japan, Indonesia, and the Jewish world, as well as the African Diaspora abroad. The imperative of diversification ranges from diversifying crops and commodities to diversifying cultures and trading partners. The struggle continues.

TOWARD INTERLOCKING PARTNERSHIPS

The fifth strategy for narrowing the Uhuru Gap is horizontal interpenetration. This involves cooperation or integration with countries on the same level of development. The first stage for Africa is Pan-Africanism — an African quest for solidarity with other African countries and with people of African descent scattered around the world.[27]

Kenya was not yet independent when the Organization of African Unity (OAU, now AU) was formed in Addis Ababa in May 1963. Mzee Jomo Kenyatta asked Oginga Odinga to represent Kenya at the meeting of the African heads of state that initiated the OAU. It fell upon Oginga Odinga to introduce to the Addis Ababa meeting the joint statement of African countries still struggling for independence at that time. Oginga Odinga felt greatly honored to speak not just for Kenya, but also for the rest of Africa that was still struggling to be free. For such countries, the feeling of "not yet Uhuru" was still very acute. Arising out of their statement to the Organization of African Unity, the Committee of Liberation was established to give support to the anticolonial struggle still raging, and to the struggle against apartheid and white minority rule in South Africa.

Pan-Africanism was not simply about the African continent. It was also about the Diaspora of African descent scattered around the world. Partly because Jomo Kenyatta and Kwame Nkrumah had studied abroad, they were much more in tune with the rest of the Black world than Oginga Odinga could claim to be. After all, both Kenyatta and Nkrumah had attended the Fifth Pan-African Congress in Manchester, England, in 1945. It turned out to be a historic Pan-African event, attended not only by Kenyatta and Nkrumah, but also by such other historic Black figures as W. E. B. DuBois of the United States and George Padmore of the West Indies.[28]

The different levels of Pan-Africanism included Trans-Saharan solidarity. This involved the unity of both Black and Arab Africans. Oginga Odinga saluted as his heroes Kwame Nkrumah, Nelson Mandela, and Gamal Abdel Nasser—arguably the towering triumvirate of Trans-Saharan Pan-Africanism.

But in his interviews with the late Odera Oruka, Oginga Odinga did not cite any single Diaspora African as one of his heroes. He did not mention as a hero Marcus Garvey of Jamaica, as Nkrumah had repeatedly done. Odinga did not cite Sylvester Williams, W. E. B. DuBois, or even Toussaint Louverture of the Haitian revolution of 1804.

It is worth bearing in mind that the African Diaspora has a number of dimensions.[29] The sovereign African Diaspora consists of those countries outside Africa whose populations are mainly of African descent, and who are currently sovereign independent countries. Such countries include Jamaica, Haiti, Barbados, and other Caribbean countries that are both sovereign and mainly Black.[30]

The concept of mega-Diaspora applies to those African Diaspora populations that are not a majority in their pluralistic sovereign countries, but whose numbers are massive. These mega-Diasporas include Black Brazil, which, after Nigeria, is rightly described as the largest Black country in the world. Depending upon one's calculation, half the population of Brazil carries African blood.[31] Black America is also part of the mega-Diaspora. With a population of some 41.7 million, Black Americans are almost three times the population of world Jewry.[32]

The third concept is that of dual diaspora. This encompasses countries populated by at least two distinct Diasporas. Guyana in South America is one such dual diaspora. Trinidad and Tobago in the West Indies is another. Each of these countries is populated both by people originally from India and by people originally from Africa—a dual diaspora, indeed.

It has been estimated that people of African ancestry who live outside Africa add up to the staggering number of 150 million people, scattered across the world, but particularly concentrated in the Western hemisphere.[33] The converging relationship between Africa and the African Diaspora adds up to what is now increasingly referred to as "Global Africa."

But horizontal interpenetration as a strategy for narrowing the Uhuru Gap goes beyond global Pan-Africanism. Africa's relationship with other developing countries can contribute to mutual liberation. Afro-Asian solidarity movements and the Non-Aligned Movement have historically linked Africa with other developing societies. And Latin American countries like Cuba and Brazil have played significant roles in Africa's postcolonial history.

During the concluding years of British rule in Kenya, Oginga Odinga did have some limited contact with Jawaharlal Nehru, India's first prime minister after its own independence in 1947. Oginga Odinga toured India in 1953 and met personally "the great Jawaharlal Nehru," as Odinga himself described him. Subsequently, Nehru provided KANU with a leading Indian constitutional lawyer (Mr. B. Malik) to help KANU formulate what it would like to see in the constitution of a self-governing Kenya.[34]

Nehru died less than a year after Kenya's independence. Oginga Odinga described Nehru as "the Chou En Lai of India" (Oruka, 1992, p. 91). Oginga intended that to be a high compliment to Nehru, although I am not sure if Nehru himself would have regarded it as complimentary! While Ghana's Kwame Nkrumah and Zambia's Kenneth Kaunda had regarded Mahatma Gandhi as their supreme Indian hero, Oginga Odinga and Uganda's Milton Obote were more fascinated by Jawaharlal Nehru.

Since Nehru's death, ideological solidarity between India and Africa has declined, but other relationships have flowered. Scholars from India have taught at various African universities; Indian engineers are now in great demand; Africans sometimes choose to go to India for complicated surgery rather than going to Europe. Economic relations between India and Africa have also grown.

Although India is only one country, while Africa has more than fifty states, the population of India is about 20 percent higher than the whole of Africa. What is more, India is on its way toward becoming the most populous country in the world—outstripping China in population in another twenty to thirty years. Oginga Odinga was justified to have taken both India and China seriously as far back as the 1950s.[35] He sensed quite early that the Uhuru Gap can best be narrowed in solidarity with others.

TOWARD COUNTERPENETRATING THE WEST

After horizontal interpenetration, the sixth strategy of ultimate decolonization is the strategy of vertical counterpenetration. Under this heading,
less-developed countries seek to counterpenetrate the citadels of power
in the industrialized world. A dramatic recent example is the rise of
Barack Obama to the presidency of the United States. This descendant of
Victoria Nyanza was first elected to the Senate of the United States in the
elections of 2004. His father was an ethnic compatriot of Oginga Odinga
and a national compatriot of all Kenyans. Yet this Kenyan-American is
only the third Black person to serve in the United States Senate in a
hundred years, and only the fifth Black senator of the United States in
two hundred years, and now the first Black president of the United
States.[36] A relatively recent descendant of a Nyanza Kenyan has counterpenetrated the citadel of governmental power in America.

Other people of African descent who have counterpenetrated the
American political system include Colin Powell, who served as the first
Black secretary of state, and Condoleezza Rice who has been the most
powerful Black woman in the world since she joined the administration
of President George W. Bush in 2001.

In the scientific and scholarly fields, counterpenetration includes the
role of African professionals in Western Europe and the United States.[37]
During the colonial period, I personally was taught by several British
teachers (male and female) in our secondary school in Mombasa in the
1940s. I did not know at that time that I would grow up to teach British
students in England and American students on their own campuses for
several decades after the colonial period. I was an African product of
Western teachers before I subsequently became an African producer of
Western graduates. My latter role was part of Africa's intellectual
counterpenetration of the Western world.

As a young man, Oginga Odinga went to much more distinguished
secondary schools than I did. Oginga went to Maseno and Alliance High
Schools, while I went to the Arab School of Mombasa. In reality, my
school was a school for Coastal Muslims, both Arab and African, but
excluding Asian Muslims. The Arab School was no match for Alliance
High School in quality. But Oginga Odinga had less of a role in counter-
penetrating the Western world, mainly because almost his entire educa-

tion was in Africa with very limited residential exposure to the Western world.

The main academic bond that Oginga Odinga had with me was through Makerere. We were both former Makerereans—he as a former student, and I as a former teacher at Makerere College in Kampala, Uganda. When I was a professor and dean at Makerere, I had occasion to invite Tom Mboya to come to speak to Makerere audiences. I believe Oginga Odinga came to Makerere under other auspices at a different time. As a leading East African academic institution, Makerere produced many graduates who later counterpenetrated the Western world. Many of those had listened to Tom Mboya and Oginga Odinga on campus. Among Makerere's most distinguished Kenyan exports to the Western world is, of course, Ngugi wa Thion'go, one of Africa's literary giants.

A more ominous form of counterpenetration is the military version. Before the final decades of the twentieth century less developed countries in Africa, Asia, and Latin America could be bombed or invaded by Northern powers with little military risk to the Northern countries. The Mau Mau fighters in Kenya could harass white settlers in Kenya or attempt to confront British troops in the Abadaire forests. But what Mau Mau could not do was bomb London or Birmingham in England.

Middle Eastern nationalists have now invented military counterpenetration into the citadels of power in the Western world.[38] On September 11, 2001, Middle Eastern nationalists destroyed the World Trade Center in New York, a symbol of American economic might; crashed into the Pentagon in Washington, D.C., a symbol of American military might; and planned to crash into either the White House or the Congressional buildings, symbols of American political power.[39] Such military counterpenetration was inconceivable in the 1950s. Kenya's Mau Mau warriors could not penetrate London militarily; nor could Angolan fighters counterpenetrate Lisbon with bombs.

Africa is being relentlessly drawn into this military crossfire of bombs and counterbombs between the Northern hemisphere and the Southern. Oginga Odinga did not live long enough to witness the bombing of the United States Embassy in Nairobi in 1998 when over 200 Kenyans, alongside twelve Americans, were killed by Middle Eastern terrorists.[40]

But Oginga Odinga was around much earlier when Cuba attempted to have countervailing missile power against the United States with the collaboration of the Soviet Union. Cuba's experiment in countervailing power triggered off the almost deadly missile crisis between John F. Kennedy's America and Nikita Khrushchev's Soviet Union in 1962.[41]

Oginga Odinga was convinced that the real hero of the Cuban Missile Crisis was Nikita Khrushchev, rather than John F. Kennedy. Odinga had met Khrushchev and reached this conclusion:

> It is Khrushchev, rather than John Kennedy, who saved the world from a possible nuclear exchange during the Cuban missile crisis of 1962.
>
> Kennedy was ready to strike, but Khrushchev swallowed his pride and withdrew the Soviet missiles from Cuba. If he had remained as adamant as Kennedy, who would have saved the world? (Oruka, 1992, p. 65)

The Cuban Missile Crisis of 1962 was an early attempt of countervailing power against the United States. Al-Qaeda under Osama bin Laden several decades later was the next big threat to the United States. Al-Qaeda was a purer case of military counterpenetration by the Third World than the Cuban/Soviet Missile Crisis had been.[42]

Unfortunately for Africa, the continent has now become a new kind of battlefield between Middle Eastern terrorism and American counterterrorism. There is a potential for African recruits into Al-Qaeda from countries like Sudan, Ethiopia, Egypt, northern Nigeria, Somalia, and perhaps even Kenya.[43] The United States needs to engage eastern and southern Africa more constructively if it is to contain the risk of military counterpenetration by Africans into the citadels of American power.

The struggle for vertical counterpenetration in Africa ranges from the entry of Nigerians into corporate America to the new roles of immigrant Ethiopians in the culture, language, and religion of America.[44] Counterpenetration is the attempt by less privileged countries to influence or contain the power of the mighty.

The struggle continues for the Southern hemisphere's more constructive counterpenetration of the North. The power of production is needed, rather than consumerism. The South needs to wield influence in the North—but more civilian power rather than military, more constructive influence rather than destructive. The struggle once again continues in the annals of the legacy of Oginga Odinga.

GLOBALIZATION AND THE UHURU GAP

Africa in the twenty-first century is likely to be one of the final battle-grounds of the forces of globalization—for better or for worse. The phenomenon called "globalization" has its winners and losers.[45] In the initial phases, Africa has been among the losers as it has been increasingly marginalized. Some universities in the United States have more computers than the computers available in an African country of twenty million people.[46] This has been the great digital divide. The distinction between the haves and have-nots has now coincided with the distinction between digitized and the "dig-prived." How can globalization narrow the Uhuru Gap rather than widen it?

Let us begin with the challenge of a definition. What is "globalization"? It consists of processes that lead toward global interdependence and the increasing rapidity of exchange across vast distances. The word "globalization" is itself quite new, but the actual processes toward global interdependence and exchange started centuries ago.[47]

Four forces have been major engines of globalization across time: religion, technology, economy, and empire. These have not necessarily acted separately, but often have reinforced each other. For example, the globalization of Christianity started with the conversion of Emperor Constantine I of Rome in 313. The religious conversion of an emperor started the process under which Christianity became the dominant religion not only of Europe, but also of many other societies later ruled or settled by Europeans.[48] The globalization of Islam began not with converting a ready-made empire, but with building an empire almost from scratch. The Umayyads and Abbasids put together bits of other people's empires (e.g., former Byzantine Egypt and former Zoroastrian Persia) and created a whole new civilization. The forces of Christianity and Islam sometimes clashed. In Africa the two religions have competed for the soul of a continent.[49]

Although Oginga Odinga was brought up a Christian, he distrusted European versions of Christianity, and did away with his Christian names. Oginga Odinga was not a Muslim either, but he observed the matrimonial Muslim maximum of four wives. He also fathered fifteen children, and adopted three additional ones. Oginga Odinga recognized Christianity and Islam as global forces, but he preferred socialism as a secular global ethic.

Voyages of exploration were another major stage in the process of globalization. Vasco da Gama and Christopher Columbus opened up a whole new chapter in the history of globalization. Economy and empire were the major motives. The migration of people followed. The Portuguese helped to build Fort Jesus in Mombasa. The migration of the Pilgrim fathers to America was in part a response to religious and economic imperatives in Europe. Demographic globalization reached its height in the Americas with the influx of millions of people from other hemispheres. In time, the population of the United States became a microcosm of the population of the world, for it contained immigrants from almost every society on earth. The making of America was the making of a globalized society or universal nation. South Africa had Dutch settlers three centuries ago—a potential universal nation on the African continent was initiated in South Africa.

The Industrial Revolution in Europe represents another major chapter in the history of globalization. This marriage between technology and economics resulted in previously unknown levels of productivity. Europe's prosperity whetted its appetite for new worlds to conquer. The Atlantic slave trade was accelerated, moving millions of Africans from one part of the world to another.[50] Europe's appetite also went imperial on a global scale, and one European people, the British, built the largest and most far-flung empire in human experience, most of which lasted until the end of World War II.[51] Kenya got its boundaries and its name from British imperialism.

The two world wars were themselves manifestations of globalization. The twentieth century is the only one to witness globalized warfare: during 1914–1918 and again during 1939–1945. The Cold War (1948–1989) was yet another manifestation of globalization, for it was a global power rivalry between two alliances: the North Atlantic Treaty Organization (NATO) and the Warsaw Pact.[52] While the two world wars were militarily more destructive, the Cold War was potentially the most dangerous—since it carried the risk of planetary annihilation in confrontations like the Cuban Missile Crisis. Oginga Odinga regarded Khrushchev as the savior of the human race in the Cuban crisis.

Oginga Odinga also regarded World War II as one of the forces that led to the rapid disintegration of the British Empire after the war. He believed that the nuclear age had made a world government a necessity.

The Uhuru Gap had been narrowed by World War II—only to be widened again by the nuclear age.

The final historical stage of globalization came when the Industrial Revolution was joined with the new Information Revolution. Interdependence and exchange became dramatically dependent upon the computer. The most powerful country by this time (1970s) was the United States. Pax Americana mobilized three of globalization's four engines: technology, economy, and empire. Although in the second half of the twentieth century this Pax Americana apparently did not seek to promote a particular religion, it did help to promote secularism and the ideology of the separation of church and state. On balance, the impact of Americanization probably has been harmful to religious values worldwide, whether intended or not. Americanized Hindu youth, Americanized Buddhist teenagers, or indeed Americanized Muslim youngsters in Mombasa are far less likely to be devout adherents of their faiths than their non-Americanized counterparts. The United States has been a secularizing force in Africa and elsewhere.[53]

In the new millennium the forces of globalization are likely to continue against the background of the meaning of the twentieth century in world history. As the twenty-first century has unfolded, scholars have interpreted globalization in three distinct ways: forces that are transforming the global market and creating new economic interdependency across vast distances. Africa is affected, but not centrally; forces are exploding into the information superhighway—expanding access to data and mobilizing the computer and the Internet into global service.

This tendency is marginalizing Africa. The Uhuru Gap is widening; all forces are turning the world into a global village—compressing distance, homogenizing culture, accelerating mobility, and reducing the relevance of political borders. Under this comprehensive definition, "globalization" is the gradual villagization of the world.[54] But these forces have been at work in Africa long before the trans-Atlantic slave trade.

As we have indicated, the twentieth century is the only century that had world wars—1914 to 1918, and 1939 to 1945. This was the only century that created world diplomatic institutions—the League of Nations and the United Nations (which Oginga Odinga believed needed drastic reforms). This was the only century that created a World Bank—the International Bank for Reconstruction and Development (IBRD) with the International Development Association. Like most socialists, however,

Oginga Odinga distrusted the World Bank and the International Monetary Fund. The twentieth century also issued a Universal Declaration of Human Rights, adopted by the United Nations in 1948. This was the only century that established a global university—the United Nations University in Tokyo, Japan. Some of these trends have affected Africa more deeply than others.

The twentieth century was the only century that had a world health institution—the World Health Organization (WHO). The twentieth century also created a global mechanism to moderate trade relations—the World Trade Organization (WTO). The Seattle meeting of WTO at the end of the millennium illustrated the depth of feelings about the organization.[55] This was the only century that had a part-time, self-appointed global policeman—the United States of America. And, of course, this was the only century that developed a genuine world economy—or at least a close approximation to it. Oginga Odinga was all too aware that this world economy was capitalist to the core.

Nevertheless, all these were indicators of globalization. Although the term "globalization" is indeed new, the forces that have been, as we indicated, creating it have been going on for generations. It is only now that we have realized that the forces at work have had global repercussions and sometimes have been global in scale. The creation of the African Diaspora as a result of the African slave trade turned out to be a manifestation of globalization.

But is a globalized world really a global village? The world may be globalized, but what would make it villagized? There is something missing: the compassion of the village has yet to be globalized. The world will never really become a global village until the contraction of distance is accompanied by the expansion of empathy. This could be the ultimate closing of the Uhuru Gap.

Education worldwide can have a role in that empathy creation. The rich must learn to be more sensitive to the poor; the better-endowed, to be more concerned about the less; the North, to be more just to the South. But for Africa there is no substitute for self-reliance than a long-term struggle. These are vital steps toward closing the Uhuru Gap.

Shakespeare said in *As You Like It*, "All the world's a stage." The new millennium asks this: "Is all the world a village?" A stage is a conceit; a village is authenticity. Where does Africa fit in? Perhaps through greater attention to global concerns and through greater effort at *kujitegemea* (self-dependence). Julius Nyerere's central slogan after the Arusha Declaration of 1967 was *Ujamaa na Kujitegemea*—Socialism and Self-Reliance.

Oginga Odinga was to the left of Julius Nyerere ideologically. Odinga believed that socialism would be a sham if Africa's condition continued to be *Uhuru bado kidogo* (not yet Uhuru). His struggle truly continues.

In conclusion, this chapter has been about Africa more than about Jaramogi Oginga Odinga, but his life and works have helped us understand Africa better. Oginga Odinga was convinced that the task of decolonization was not yet complete. To use Oginga's own words: "When we hang out the national flag for *Uhuru* meetings and rallies we don't want the cries of *wapi Uhuru* (where is Uhuru) to drown the cheers. Our independence struggle was not meant to enrich a minority. It was to cast off the yoke of colonialism and of poverty" (Odinga, 1967, p. 310).

In this chapter I have used the concept of *Uhuru Gap* (freedom gap) to signify the distance yet to be covered before *real Uhuru* can be achieved. Africa's independence is a work in progress. We have identified seven strategies in the quest for greater freedom. These strategies are embedded in interlocking institutions whether written or not, traditional or foreign.

Oginga Odinga was a major actor within the strategy of *democratization*. He was crucial in the struggle for a multiparty democracy. But the problem of checks and balances is posing new challenges in the era of his son, Raila Odinga.

The strategy of *domestication* involves making a foreign institution more relevant for Africa. How can the African state be made truly African? At stake are issues that range from choice of the official language of a country to a culturally relevant constitution.

The strategy of domestication overlaps with the strategy of *indigenization*. Both Odinga and Kenyatta were traditionalists. When Odinga entered Parliament in traditional African dress and sandals, he was helping to Africanize Parliament itself symbolically.

The strategy of *diversification* may include diversifying the economy or diversifying ideological options, or diversifying trading partners and aid donors. When Tom Mboya cultivated Western leaders and Oginga Oginda cultivated leaders of the Communist world, Kenya benefited from the diversity of friendships.

The strategy of *horizontal interpenetration* cultivates solidarity with societies of comparable levels of development. Oginga Odinga was less involved with Pan-Africanism than Kwame Nkrumah, Julius Nyerere, or even Jomo Kenyatta in his younger days. But there is little doubt that if Oginga had been elected president of Kenya, he would have been much more Pan-Africanist than Kenyatta's government was.

The strategy of *vertical counterpenetration* involves penetrating the citadels of power. When Africans become influential or powerful in Europe or America that is counterpenetration. When a person of Kenyan Luo descent such as Barack Obama becomes only the third Black U.S. senator in more than a hundred years, and eventually the president, that is spectacular counterpenetration.

The seventh strategy is that of *globalization*. Oginga Odinga was in many ways a globalist in the best sense of the term. He even dreamt of a world government in the future as the ultimate check on human militarism. But while Africa has suffered from some of the economic consequences of globalization, Africa also has benefited from a new global concern for the poor and the afflicted. When eight major cities of the world held concerts on live television to draw attention to the teeming millions of impoverished Africans, that was a new level of global awareness, even if the practical results in poverty alleviation are modest.[56]

When Africans become vice presidents of the World Bank or when the continent produces two secretaries-general of the United Nations back-to-back, that is a bonus of the new global awareness.

Less attractive is military counterpenetration. In the past, less-developed countries could be invaded or bombed by the great powers without the weak being able to hit at the powerful in their metropolitan cities. The Mau Mau could fight British troops on Kenyan soil but could not militarily attack the British in London or Manchester.

Oginga Odinga died before Al-Qaeda counterpenetrated the United States on September 11, 2001, and demolished the World Trade Center and part of the Pentagon. Unlike Mau Mau fighters, Middle Eastern nationalists of today can now use terrorist methods to hit back at the most powerful cities in the world. The force of counterpenetration and the forces of globalization are generating both hope and despair in the new millennium. But Oginga Odinga remained the ultimate optimist. "If there is any reward to be gained by ending the Cold War, it should be that which follow after a truly global structure of democratic governance is put in place. . . . But it must realize that politics is about ideals; ideals that inspire people to action; ideals that spell out what is possible under difficult objective circumstances" (Oruka, 1992, pp. 138–139).

Oginga Odinga tried his best to live according to his own ideals—often at the risk of his freedom, if not his life. He was detained more than once. The Kenya electorate missed a great opportunity when they did not give him a chance to pursue his ideals from the pinnacle of power—the presidency. But, as democrats, we must submit to the will of the people. So be it.

NOTES

1. Pio Gama Pinto was a Kenyan journalist, politician, and freedom fighter. His political orientation was socialism, and he dedicated himself to Kenyan independence liberation.

2. On the two assassinations, see Keith Kyle, *The Politics of the Independence of Kenya* (New York: St. Martin's Press in association with Institute of Contemporary British History, 1999), pp. 202–203.

3. On the rivalry, see Kyle's 1999 *The Politics of the Independence of Kenya*, pp. 85–86.

4. In an address to the Houston Ministerial Association on September 12, 1960, candidate John Kennedy laid out his case to the American public, summing up his argument in these famous words:

> I do not speak for my church on public matters—and the church does not speak for me. Whatever issue may come before me as president—on birth control, divorce, censorship, gambling or any other subject—I will make my decision in accordance with these views, in accordance with what my conscience tells me to be the national interest, and without regard to outside religious pressures or dictates. And no power or threat of punishment could cause me to decide otherwise. (Avella and McKeown, eds., *Public Voices: Catholics in the American Context* [Maryknoll, NY: Orbis Books, 1999], p. 363)

5. There were various oaths at different levels; for descriptions and analyses, consult Wunyabari Maloba, *Mau Mau and Kenya: An Analysis of a Peasant Revolt* (Bloomington: Indiana University Press, 1993), pp. 102–109; and Marshall S. Clough, *Mau Mau Memoirs: History, Memory, and Politics* (Boulder, CO: Lynne Rienner Publishers, 1998), pp. 98–99.

6. Consult John Iliffe, "The Organization of the Maji Maji Rebellion," and Patrick M. Redmond, "Maji Maji in Ungoni: A Reappraisal of Existing Historiography," in *Conquest and Resistance to Colonialism in Africa*, ed. Gregory Maddox (New York: Garland, 1993), pp. 217–252.

7. Relatedly, see T. O. Ranger, "Connexions between 'Primary Resistance' and Modern Nationalism in East and Central Africa, Parts I and II," *Journal of African History* 9 (1968): pp. 437–53 and pp. 631–41.

8. The British did not give up their colony in Kenya without a struggle and grievous violations of human rights. See, for some analyses, Caroline Elkins, *Imperial Reckoning: The Untold Story of Britain's Gulag in Kenya* (New York: Henry Holt, 2005); and David Anderson, *Histories of the Hanged: The Dirty War in Kenya and the End of Empire* (New York: W. W. Norton, 2005).

9. Indeed, in a letter to Churchill dated July 17, 1944, Gandhi wrote:

> Dear Prime Minister,
> You are reported to have the desire to crush the "naked fakir," as you are said to have described me. I have been long trying to be a fakir and that, naked—a more difficult task. I therefore regard the expression as a compliment though unintended. I approach you then as such and ask you to trust and use me for the sake of your people and mine and through them those of the world.
> Your sincere friend,
> M. K. GANDHI

The letter is reprinted in Ministry of Information and Broadcasting, *Collected Works of Mahatma Gandhi*, Volume 77 (New Delhi and Ahmedabad: Government of India and the Navajivan Trust, 1979), p. 391.

10. This famous line is from the play *Hamlet,* Act I, Scene III.

11. Oginga was an exception among the Kenyan leaders in wearing African attire, according to B. A. Ogot and W. R. Ochieng', eds., *Decolonization and Independence in Kenya* (London: James Currey and Athens; Ohio University Press, 1995), p. 147. For some general discussions on the significance of political expression through attire in Africa, also consult Jean Allman, ed., *Fashioning Africa: Power and the Politics of Dress* (Bloomington: Indiana University Press, 2004).

12. See Ogot and Ochieng', 1995, *Decolonization and Independence in Kenya*, p. 108 and p. 139.

13. For a discussion of this custom, consult R. G. Abraham, "Some Aspects of Levirate," in *The Character of Kinship*, ed. Jack Goody (Cambridge: Cambridge University Press, 1973), pp. 163–74.

14. This critique has been explored in detail by Ndirangu Mwaura in *Kenya Today: Breaking the Yoke of Colonialism in Africa* (New York: Algora Publishing, 2005), pp. 171–85.

15. Majimbo in Swahili means "regions" and it refers to devolution of political power to the regions.

16. Indeed, one study posits that the failure of federalism in Africa, when compared to the American experience, may be the lack of concern for minority rights. See Edmond J. Keller and Barbara Thomas-Woolley, "Majority Rules and Minority Rights: American Federalism and African Experience," *Journal of Modern African Studies* 32 (3, September 1994): pp. 411–27. For another discussion of federalism as an answer to African ethnic problems, see Mwangi S. Kimenyi, "Harmonizing Ethnic Claims in Africa: A Proposal for Ethnic-Based Federalism," *CATO Journal* 18 (1, Spring/Summer 1998): pp. 43–64.

17. Discussions of the state of federalism in Nigeria can be found in Rotimi T. Suberu, "Nigeria: Dilemmas of Federalism," in *Federalism and Territorial Cleavages*, eds. Ugo M. Amoretti and Nancy Bermeo (Baltimore, MD: Johns Hopkins University Press, 2004), pp. 327–54; and also see Rotimi T. Suberu, *Federalism and Ethnic Conflict in Nigeria* (Washington, DC: United States Institute of Peace Press, 2001).

18. For Oginga Odinga's interpretation of the KANU-KADU equilibrium, see his book *Not Yet Uhuru*, especially chapters 11 and 12 (New York: Hill and Wang, 1967), pp. 193–231. See also H. Odera Oruka, ed., *Oginga Odinga: His Philosophy and Beliefs* (Nairobi: Initiatives Publishers), p. 96, about Luo governance.

19. In 1965 this was amended to a 65 percent majority requirement in both houses.

20. We will probably argue that this was fulfilled in the aftermath of the post-2007 election violence in Kenya. The power-sharing agreement put in place established presidential and prime ministerial positions until 2012.

21. A number of interesting historical and current material on the Kenyan constitution is available at the site http://www.kenyaconstitution.org/ (accessed August 5, 2005).

22. Consult E. S. Atieno-Odhiambo, *Jaramogi Ajuma Oginga Odinga* (Nairobi: East African Educational Publishers, 1997), p. 21, on the perception of Oginga Odinga 's and Mboya's international orientations.

23. A detailed description of the airlift can be found in David Goldsworthy, *Tom Mboya: The Man Kenya Wanted to Forget* (New York: Africana Publishing Company, 1982), pp. 166–69.

24. For a report about the rise and fall of the Lumumba Institute in Kenya, see John Kamau's article "How Kenya's Best Kept Secret Became a Hotbed of Insurgents," *Sunday Standard* (Nairobi), July 11, 2004.

25. A television series on this theme was broadcast on the BBC and PBS, among others; the companion volume to the series is Ali A. Mazrui, *The Africans: A Triple Heritage* (Boston: Little, Brown, 1986).

26. See N. Mwaura, *Kenya Today: Breaking the Yoke of Colonialism in Africa* (New York: Algora Publishing, 2005), pp. 171–85.

27. Useful works on Pan-Africanism include Michael W. Williams, *Pan-Africanism: An Annotated Bibliography* (Pasadena, CA: Salem Press, 1992); and for an overview, see P. Olisanwuche Esedebe, *Pan-Africanism: The Idea and Movement, 1776–1991*, 2nd ed. (Washington, DC: Howard University, 1994).

28. For descriptions of this important conference, see Darryl C. Thomas, *The Theory and Practice of Third World Solidarity* (Westport, CT: Praeger, 2001), p. 155; Manning Marable, *Black Leadership* (New York: Columbia University Press, 1998), pp. 94–95; and Esedebe, 1994, *Pan-Africanism*, pp. 138–46.

29. Both general and specific discussions on African Diasporas can be found, for example, in the following: Joseph E. Harris, ed. *Global Dimensions of the African Diaspora*, 2nd ed. (Washington, DC: Howard University Press, 2003); Shihan De Silva Jayasuriya and Richard Pankhurst, eds., *The African Diaspora in the Indian* Ocean (Trenton, NJ: Africa World Press, 2003); Erna Brodber, *The Continent of Black Consciousness: On the History of the African Diaspora from Slavery to the Present Day* (London: New Beacon Books, 2003); John Hunwick and Eve T. Powell, *The African Diaspora in the Mediterranean Lands of Islam* (Princeton, NJ: Markus Wiener Publishers, 2002); Darlene Clark Hine and Jacqueline McLeod., eds., *Crossing Boundaries: Comparative History of Black People in Diaspora* (Bloomington: Indiana University Press, 1999); E. L. Bute, *The Black Handbook: The People, History and Politics of Africa and the African Diaspora* (London: Cassell, 1997); Alusine Jalloh and Stephen E. Maizlish, eds., *The African Diaspora* (College Station: Texas A&M University Press, 1996); Michael L. Conniff and Thomas J. Davis, *Africans in the Americas: A History of the Black Diaspora* (New York: St. Martin's Press, 1994); and Edward Scobie, *Global African Presence* (Brooklyn, NY: A & B Books, 1994).

30. According to figures compiled on the basis of the *2009 1 CIA World Factbook*, the total population of the Caribbean was 39.17 million and at least 65 percent of that total were Black or people of African descent.

31. See, for example, Abdias do Nascimento, "Blacks and Politics in Brazil," in *Africana: The Encyclopedia of the African and African American Experience*, 2nd ed., eds.

Kwame Anthony Appiah, Henry Louis Gates, Jr. (Oxford and New York: Oxford University Press, 2005), 1: p. 619.

32. The figure for Black Americans is on the basis of a report from the U.S. Census Bureau, estimating U.S. population levels as of July 1, 2010; see Robert Pear, "Ethnic Minorities Gain in the Nation as a Whole," *New York Times*, August 12, 2005. The number of Jews worldwide was estimated at 14.4 million; see John W. Storey and Glenn H. Utter, *Religion and Politics: A Reference Handbook*, (Santa Barbara, CA: ABC-CLIO, 2002), p. 119.

33. In addition to the nearly 42 million African Americans in North America, figures compiled from the *2010 population census CIA World Factbook* show that, of the estimated 490 million people in Latin America, when the classification of a Black person in the United States is used, there were at least 90 million (18.5 percent) Blacks in that region, and close to 24 million in the Caribbean.

34. Odinga, Ogonda. 1967, *Not Yet Uhuru*, pp. 128–29, 222.

35. Relatedly, consult Clyde Prestowitz, *Three Billion New Capitalists: The Great Shift of Wealth and Power to the East* (New York: Basic Books, 2005).

36. Barack Obama coasted to a victory for the Illinois Senate seat in the 2004 elections and made an electrifying speech at the Democratic Convention that year. For a report on the speech, see David Broder, "Democrats Focus on Healing Divisions: Addressing Convention, Newcomers Set Themes," *The Washington Post*, July 28, 2004, p. 1.; and for an early analysis of his attractiveness to voters, see Scott L. Malcomson, "An Appeal beyond Race," *The New York Times*, August 1, 2004.

37. For instance, according to a March 28, 2003, speech by United States Deputy Assistant Secretary of State, Pamela E. Bridgewater, "There are now more than 250,000 scientists and physicians of African descent in the United States." See Pamela E. Bridgewater, "The African Diaspora and Its Influence on African Development," speech delivered at Kentucky State University, March 28, 2003, http://usembassy-australia.state.gov/hyper/2003/0403/epf410.htm), accessed March 24, 2004.

38. Among those who have been recruited into this struggle are Africans; the suspects in the July 21, 2005, botched bombings in London were from Somalia, Eritrea, and Ethiopia. See Kevin Sullivan, "Attempted Murder Charges Brought in London Attack," *The Washington Post*, August 9, 2005.

39. For a gripping account of the 9/11 plot in a thriller style, consult National Commission on Terrorist Attacks upon the United States, *9/11 Commission Report: Final Report of the National Commission on Terrorist Attacks upon the United States* (New York: W. W. Norton, 2004).

40. Consult "Now for Africa," *The Economist*, July 5, 2003, p. 9; and for one report lamenting the end of the African "safe haven," see Baffour Ankomah, "Bombers Hit Africa," *New African* 367 (October 1998): pp. 16–17.

41. The world came perilously close to an end during the Cuban Missile Crisis of 1962. For updated accounts of the crisis, see, for example, Keith Eubank, *The Missile Crisis in Cuba* (Malabar, FL: Krieger Publishing Company, 2000); and James G. Blight and David A. Welch, *On the Brink: Americans and Soviets Reexamine the Cuban Missile Crisis* (New York: Hill and Wang, 1989).

42. For a quick overview of Al-Qaeda, see Anonymous, *Imperial Hubris: Why The West Is Losing the War on Terror* (Washington, DC: Brassey's, 2004), pp. 55–67; and for an extended description, see Rohan Gunaratna, *Inside Al Qaeda: Global Network of Terror* (London: Hurst & Co., 2002).

43. As mentioned before, in the July 21, London, attempted bombing case, the alleged bombers were originally from Somalia, Eritrea and Ethiopia; see Sullivan, "Attempted Murder Charges Brought in London Attack," *The Washington Post*, August 9, 2005.

44. On African immigration to the United States, see Darlington I. I. Ndubuike, *The Struggles, Challenges and Triumphs of the African Immigrant in* America (Lewiston, NY: Edwin Mellen Press, 2002); John A. Arthur, *Invisible Sojourners: African Immigrant Diaspora in the United States* (Westport, CT: Praeger, 2000); Kofi A. Apraku, *African Emigres in the United States: A Missing Link in Africa's Social and Political Development* (New York: Praeger, 1991); and April Gordon, "The New Diaspora: African Immigration to the United States," *Journal of Third World Studies* 15 (Spring 1998), pp. 79–103.

45. For some opposing views on globalization, see Jagdish Bhagwati, *In Defense of Globalization* (New York: Oxford University Press, 2004); and Joseph E. Stiglitz, *Globalization and Its Discontents* (New York: W. W. Norton, 2003).

46. Statistics on the number of computers by country are available at the website of the International Telecommunications Union at http://www.itu.int/ITU-D/ict/statistics/at_glance/Internet03.pdf (accessed November 15, 2004); the Congo had 15,000 computers, according to that source.

47. For some discussions on globalization consult Mohammed A. Bamyeh, *The Ends of Globalization* (Minneapolis: University of Minnesota Press, 2000); Mark Rupert, *Ideologies of Globalization: Contending Visions of a New World Order* (London and New York: Routledge, 2000); and Colin Hays and David Marsh, eds., *Demystifying Globalization* (New York: St. Martin's Press in association with Polsis, University of Birmingham, 2000).

48. For a discussion of the impact of Constantine on Christianity, see Christopher B. Coleman, *Constantine the Great and Christianity, Three Phases: The Historical, The Legendary, and the Spurious* (New York: Columbia University Press, 1914).

49. Relatedly, consult Jeff Haynes, ed., *Religion, Globalization and Political Culture in the Third World* (New York: St. Martin's Press, 2000).

50. A comprehensive analysis of the slave trade can be found in Joseph E. Inikori and Stanley L. Engerman, eds., *The Atlantic Slave Trade: Effects on Economies and Peoples in Africa, the Americas, and Europe* (Durham, NC: Duke University Press, 1992).

51. For a history of the British Empire, see P. J. Marshall, ed., *The Cambridge Illustrated History of the British Empire* (New York: Cambridge University Press, 2001).

52. For treatments of the Cold War consult, for instance, Lori L. Bogle, ed. *The Cold War* (New York: Routledge, 2001); and Francis J. Gavin, ed., *The Cold War* (Chicago: Fitzroy Dearborn Publishers, 2001).

53. Of course, the homogenizing impulse of American culture has also invoked local revolts; in this vein, see relatedly, Benjamin Barber, *Jihad vs. McWorld* (New York: Times Books, 1995).

54. On this aspect, see Marshall McLuhan and Bruce R. Powers, *The Global Village: Transformations in World Life and Media in the 21st Century* (New York: Oxford University Press, 1989).

55. For one analysis of the causes of discontent with the Seattle meeting and WTO, see Nicholas Bayne, "Why Did Seattle Fail? Globalization and the Politics of Trade," *Government and Opposition* 35 (2, Spring 2000), pp. 131–51.

56. For some African reactions to the Live 8 concerts, see Jean-Claude Shanda Tonme, "All Rock, No Action," *The New York Times*, July 15, 2005; and Gebreselassie Y. Tesfamichael, "In Africa, Just Help Us to Help Ourselves," *The Washington Post*, July 24, 2005.

EIGHT

"Katiba Na Kabila"

If African Politics Are Ethnic Prone, Can African Constitutions Be Ethnic Proof?

Ali A. Mazrui

Ethnicity plays a fundamental role within African societies. It has structured and defined societal organizations, beliefs, and progress within societies. On the other hand, primordialists have also argued for the negative consequences of ethnicity, including the onset of conflict. Thus, ethnicity as an institution impacts the nature of African societies. However, despite the key role ethnicity plays in African societies, less effort in both research and government policies has gone into incorporating ethnic realities into constitutions of African states.

This chapter discusses ethnicity and state constitutions in Africa. It asks whether African states' constitutions should be ethnic proof? There is no doubt that African constitutions need to recognize the reality that ethnicity is embedded in the sociocultural and political fabrics of African societies. Though not extensively discussed in the literature, ethnic marginalization could be described as one of the grave civil rights abuses within African societies. African societies struggle to deal with ethnic tensions and marginalization and this suggests an intentional and pragmatic approach to dealing with the problem. As constitutions are becoming legitimate referent points in democratic transitions in Africa, an ethnic-proof constitution is a starting point to address ethnic marginaliza-tion and tensions.

The fundamental objective of a constitution is to provide transparency by acting as a term of reference. Constitutions not only force elites to be accountable for their actions within the constitutional framework, but also serve as a referent point where citizens can challenge elites when they operate outside the framework. Thus an open society is encouraged leading to a just and equitable social order.

When in my television series *The Africans: A Triple Heritage* I accused Kaiser Aluminum of having exploited Ghana, the multinational corpora-tion threatened legal action unless that accusation was deleted from the TV series. We consulted with my television producers' lawyers and my own lawyers in the United States as to whether Kaiser Aluminum could stop me from accusing them of the exploitation of Ghana. All the American lawyers were unanimous: Kaiser Aluminum would not stand a chance under U.S. law. We therefore went ahead and showed the TV series in the United States without deleting my accusation. Kaiser de-cided discretion was the better part of valor. They did not take legal action.

In the United States the law was on the side of the open society. In Kenya, on the other hand, the law of libel can be used to stop the flow of information, rather than to facilitate it. Libel law in Kenya can be an ally of censorship rather than a partner of an open society. In August of 2001 the courts in Kenya twice intervened on the side of interrupting the flow of information in the case of President Moi's son and the serialization of Smith Hempstone's memoirs.

Dealing with ethnicity and constitutions, one of the questions that needs to be addressed is whether the future Constitution of Kenya needs a Freedom of Information Clause. Or are there alternative democratic means of promoting the democratic goal of open society? As discussed in the previous chapter, four fundamental goals of democracy include mak-ing political elites accountable and answerable for their actions and poli-cies, making ordinary citizens effective participants in the process of choosing their leaders and in regulating their leaders' actions, making the society and economy as open and transparent as possible, and making the social order fundamentally just and equitable to the majority of the people.

Achieving these goals requires different means. Some countries such as the United States have chosen separation of powers and checks and balances to force political elites to be more accountable, while others such the United Kingdom have embraced the idea of sovereignty of parliament. Thus there are different means by which the executive branch could be made accountable for the use of its power.[1]

If the goals of democracy are the same, while the means for achieving them differ, are there African means of achieving those same four goals of accountability of rulers, participation of citizens, openness of society, and greater social justice? The challenge facing constitution makers in Africa is how to keep the democratic goals constant while looking for a more appropriate democratic means.

It is in the light of this that one canon of African political discourse and narrative—ethnicity—become relevant in Africa's democratization process and consolidation. Primordialists have argued that the fundamental cause of most conflicts in Africa is ethnicity. Some have even suggested that depluralizing societies could help stabilize states and create the conditions for development.[2] It is clear that the modern state system and precolonial political systems have not been properly reconciled in Africa. There is a disconnect in the transition. Thus many of the means of achieving democratic consolidation have merely been trial and error. Though ethnicity influences the nature of African societies, there has not been any effort to incorporate ethnicity into the African constitution. The argument here is not advocating for a consociational form of political system, but that by injecting ethnicity into the constitution, a cultural reality is accounted for as a pragmatic means of achieving democracy.

THE IRON LAW OF ETHNIC LOYALTY

One major characteristic of politics in postcolonial Africa is that they are ethnic prone. My favorite illustration from Kenya's postcolonial history was Oginga Odinga's efforts to convince Kenyans that they had not yet achieved Uhuru, but were being taken for a ride by corrupt elite and their foreign backers. Oginga Odinga called upon underprivileged Kenyans to follow him toward a more just society. When Oginga Odinga looked to see who was following him, it was not all underprivileged Kenyans regardless of ethnic group but fellow Luo regardless of social classes.[3] It was not the song of social justice that attracted his followers; it was who the singer was—a distinguished Luo. Not the message, but the messenger.

In Nigeria another powerful illustration of Africa's Iron Law of Ethnicity concerned the late Obafemi Awolowo. He too called upon Nigerians to follow him toward a new and more just "Jerusalem." When Awolowo looked to see who was following him, he saw not underprivileged Nigerians of all ethnic groups, but fellow Yoruba regardless of class. It was not the song, but the singer that mattered; it was not the message, but the messenger.

The ethnic proneness of African politics affects not only who is elected, but also how jobs are allocated and it affects the triumph of ethnic nepotism as one branch of corruption. Power plays, capital transfers, loyalties and solidarities, jobs and opportunities, scholarships and bursaries, loans and gifts—all are influenced to one degree or another by the pervasive power of ethnicity in Africa.

In Kenya, whoever becomes president can help his home district or province enormously in development and enhancement of the infrastructure. Nairobi and the Central Province gained a lot in institutional development during the Kenyatta years; the Rift Valley gained a lot during the Moi years.

Strangely enough Northern Uganda gained very little during the years of Milton Obote and Idi Amin although they belonged to Northern "tribes." Similarly Northern Nigeria benefited less than it should have done during the long years of Northern military dominance. There is therefore one thing worse than a president who favors his own district— and that is a president who totally neglects his district and just favors his own pocket.

One ethnic check that has been suggested in countries like Nigeria (and indeed Kenya) is a regionally rotating presidency. Nigeria usually had Muslim heads of states coming repeatedly from the North. One solution was a constitutional provision for regional or zonal rotation of the presidency. Moshood Abiola would have been an ideal rotation without a constitutional provision—another Muslim president, but this one from Southern Nigeria. Nigeria also had Olusegun Obasanjo, a non-Muslim Southerner. A rotation has occurred without a constitutional provision.

Another ethnic check that both Nigeria and Kenya have tried out is to require that a president not be electable unless he or she has a minimum of multiprovincial support; it is not enough that a head of state has a majority of the people on his or her side. That majority must also be distributed nationally. Perhaps the president should demonstrate support in at least one quarter of the provinces. Nigerians and Kenyans are already familiar with this kind of safeguard against an ethnic-specific head of state.

One idea has not been pursued in Africa: Can we have a multiparty parliament combined with a no-party executive president? Can we have a constitution in which candidates for president belong to no political party and are required to be nonpartisan as executive heads of state—while parliament operates on the basis of a multiparty competition? This would enable the head of state to be truly above the interparty squabbles and attain a higher level of political objectivity. The Kenyan president would not be a member of KANU or FORD or the Democratic Party or any other party. He or she would be above the fray.

The disadvantage of this system is that only the very rich individual candidates would be able to launch a presidential campaign without the support of party functionaries all over the country.

INSTITUTIONAL CHECKS AND ETHNIC BALANCES

We mentioned earlier that the democratic goal of making the government more accountable has in Britain involved the democratic means of sovereignty of parliament, and in the United States, the democratic means of checks and balances. Can Africa find new democratic means that combine a new concept of the sovereignty of parliament and an even newer concept of checks and balances?

In most of sub-Saharan Africa the challenge lies in finding ethnic checks and balances that are appropriate and effective, and combining them with gender checks and balances. Both ethnic and gender checks and balances have the potential to enhance Africa's drive to sustainable and consolidated democracy.

Ignoring ethnicity in constitutional documents in Africa demonstrates a blatant disregard for a fundamental knit of the society.[4] Over the years, African governments, be they civilian or military, have deferred to the people of their own ethnicities for support and trust to rule. The ideal and pragmatic governing principle would have been an ethnic-neutral strategy. However, time and again, the power of ethnicity has overwhelmed political elites as they try to mobilize the society to a common goal of nation building.

Though an appreciable number of states in Africa have understood the importance of women in nation building and making efforts to involve women in political decision making, many obstacles still exist in the way of women in achieving their full potential. These two significant aspects of African societies have affected the continent's drive to create strong democracies. The failure to consider these significant phenomena within African societies hinders their political and economic development.

I was in Ghana in the early 2000s. On that visit I was graciously received by the Asantehene (Otumfuo Nana Osei Tutu II), the King of Ashanti. At the time, he was a newly installed Asantehene, chosen by the elders, always in consultation with a personage called the "Queen Mother." The term "Queen Mother" in Ashanti—unlike in Britain—is not a biological relationship; it is an official title with an official role. In other words, in Ashanti traditional society, a high female personage is always involved in choosing who the next king is going to be. This female role carries immense influence and power.

When we are drawing up new constitutions in Africa we almost never consult the traditional constitutions of precolonial Africa.[5] How many constitutional commissions in Africa have bothered to find out how Ashanti was ruled, or how the Kikuyu governed themselves before colonial rule, or how precolonial Somali achieved the miracle of having rules without having rulers, the miracle of ordered anarchy.[6]

We do not have to repeat exactly what the Ashanti, or the precolonial Kikuyu or Somali did. What is needed is simply to learn from them, and perhaps adopt some of their ideas. For example, how do we get a Queen Mother into the Kenya system? The office of the speaker of Parliament could always be occupied by a woman.[7] That is one option. A modified version is to make the position of speaker alternate between a man and a woman. If the present speaker is a man, the next one has to be a woman regardless of the party in power. Another possible Queen Mother scenario in a modern context is to have two vice presidents—one a man and the other a woman, from two different ethnic groups, and both ethnically different from the president.

Africa has experimented before with racial checks and balances—as in Kenya's Legislative Council in the 1950s with representatives of different racial groups, and Zimbabwe after independence in the 1980s when there were reserved seats for Europeans. Lebanon has a constitution of religious checks and balances: the president has to be a Maronite Christian; the prime minister has to be a Sunni Muslim; the Speaker of the National Assembly has to be Shiite Muslim; and the different religious denominations have prescribed percentages of parliamentary seats. According to the National Pact of Lebanon of 1943, the distribution of the parliamentary seats was six Christians to every five Muslims. But the religious population in the wider society has shifted in favor of Muslims. This was a major cause of the Lebanese civil war. The Taif Accord of 1990 attempted some kind of parity.[8]

On attainment of independence Kenya had a majimbo[9] constitution that was an experiment in ethnic checks and balances. Though this ethnically based autonomous governance was floated around the time of independence, major political parties such as the Orange Democratic Movement (ODM) led by Raila Odinga were in full support of this system during the 2007 election campaign. In reality all sub-Saharan African countries should have started experimenting with constitutions partially based on ethnic checks and balances.

Instead most African countries behaved as if they were ready-made nation-states in full bloom as unitary states. No effort was made on the part of the African political elites to reexamine the nature of the African state and its political institutions at the time of independence. As a result of this, civil wars and other unstable conditions within African societies could be interpreted as lingering struggles against existing colonial structures.[10] "Federalism" was almost a dirty word virtually everywhere outside Nigeria. Nor did federalism work in Nigeria since the country was under military rule most of the time since independence.[11]

This failure to construct viable ethnic checks and balances cost hundreds of thousands of lives in Rwanda, Uganda, Burundi, Sudan, the Congo, Nigeria, and elsewhere. Kenya may not need the kind of complicated majimbo promulgated at the time of independence in 1963, but some degree of devolution of power to the provinces is needed to avert internal colonialism by those who control centralized power in Nairobi.

Creating a system of ethnic checks and balances has often been confused with the quest for the detribalization or de-ethnicization of politics. The system of ethnic checks and balances accepts the legitimacy of the ethnic factor in politics. It only tries to channel it into areas of constructive accommodation and fairness.

On the other hand, the quest for de-ethnicization of politics often treats ethnicity and tribalism as political pathologies. Many African policy makers have been in a state of denial about the reality of political ethnicity.

The old one-party state in Kenya, Tanzania, and Ghana was one method that was indeed tried out to de-ethnicize politics (or depoliticize ethnicity). It was widely assumed (not without reason) that competitive multiparty politics activates ethnic rivalries and can be destabilizing. One African country after another invoked the one-party state, as a bulwark against ethnic tensions.

Yoweri Museveni's governing era of No-Party State[12] in Uganda between 1995 and 2005 was another experiment in de-ethnicizing politics. Museveni has argued persuasively that the multiparty system in Uganda in the past has often ignited not only ethnic rivalry, but also downright conflict. The 2005 constitutional referendum reversed this, allowing for active political activities by political parties. Currently we have the National Resistance Movement (NRM) that is the governing party, Conservative Party, Democratic Party, Forum for Democratic Change, and Federal Democratic Party, among others, operating in Uganda. In reality Museveni has allowed a good deal of multiparty rhetoric and debate and party labels. What he has not permitted is multiparty organization and mobilization. The central concern has been fear of ethnic violence.

Milton Obote's first administration had a concept that was more than just de-ethnicization of politics. Obote was on his way toward a real concept of ethnic checks and balances. What I have in mind is what was known in 1970 as Document No. 5 of Milton Obote's (1968–1971) Move to the Left. He envisaged every parliamentary candidate as having four constituencies—one primary one and three subsidiary ones. If the primary one was in the east, the subsidiary ones could be in the west, north and south. And so on and so forth.

Each candidate would need a plurality of votes in his or her primary constituency, and a particular minimum percentage of votes in the three subsidiary constituencies. The idea was to force each parliamentary candidate to campaign for support from among northerners, southerners, westerners, as well as his or her primary easterners (if indeed east was the primary constituency).

Obote's first administration did not last long enough to implement this Document No. 5 of what was teasingly called "Electoral Polygamy"—one candidate with four constituencies. Milton Obote was overthrown by Idi Amin Dada in January 1971 on the eve of the proposed implementation of Document No. 5.

If one candidate standing for four constituencies is too many constituencies, how about one candidate standing for just two constituencies—one primary one that may be of his or her own ethnic group, and the other constituency distant from his roots? The candidate has to learn how to court voters of divergent ethnic backgrounds.

TOWARD GENDER CHECKS AND BALANCES

While the case for ethnic checks and balances is ultimately to avert the destructiveness of ethnic conflict, the case for gender checks and balances is ultimately to promote greater androgynous creativity and development. Happy ethnic relations are necessary because the alternative is the danger of devastation. Better gender relations are necessary because the alternative is waste of talent, as well as injustice.

The ultimate developmental case for ethnic checks and balances is to avert destruction. The ultimate developmental case for gender checks and balances is to promote innovation and creativity. Of course, gender equity is also an issue of human rights in the moral sphere.

In parliamentary constitutional reform, there is the need for gender reservation of seats. The 2010 constitutional reform in Kenya allocated a minimum of forty-seven seats for women, which meant that each of the forty-seven counties should at least nominate a female to the lower house. Gender equity has implications for religious beliefs. With the wave of Islamic extremism including Al Qaeda, Taliban, and Boko Haram against female education, the debate needs to focus on Kenyan Muslims' support for such gender equity in politics. Kenyan Muslims should remember that in some aspects of female empowerment, the Muslim world is ahead of most of the Western world.

In the last quarter century four different Muslim countries have had female heads of state or heads of government. It started with Pakistan where Benazir Bhutto was prime minister twice. There followed Bangladesh, another country with a large Muslim population. In Bangladesh both the ruling party and the opposition have been led by women—

Sheikh Hasina Wajed and Begum Khaleda Zea. Turkey, a Muslim society with a secular state, has had Mrs. Tansu Çiller as prime minister.

The largest Muslim country in population—Indonesia—had a Muslim female president, Megawati Sukarnoputri, from July 2001 to October 2004. All this has been happening in the Muslim world long before the United States has had even a female vice president, let alone a female head of government. Germany now has a female Chancellor, Angela Merkel, and even the Islamic Republic of Iran has had at least a woman deputy president.

Four Muslim countries have therefore already experienced years when the most powerful single individual in the land has been a woman. This is the Muslim equivalent of the Ashanti Queen Mother writ really large, even more than a king maker, but a female Paramount head.

The legacy of our Lady Aisha, as a political woman, is not to be found today within the boundaries of where she was born fourteen centuries ago. The torch of Lady Aisha, the Prophet's politicized widow, has been passed to the Muslims farther east—in Islamabad, in Dacca, in Kuala Lumpur, and in Jakarta.

Just as those Muslims of South and Southeast Asia have led the West in ultimate female empowerment, Muslims of Kenya should similarly lead the way in helping to empower the women of Kenya of all faiths. Here in Africa, as in Asia, the stereotype glass that portrays Islam as the most antiwomen of all world religions needs to be shattered. The evidence of history contradicts such stereotypes, and we should be on the correct side of history.

TOWARD MUSLIM AND COASTAL EMPOWERMENT

What about the status of the Coast province of Kenya itself? In a lecture I delivered in Mombasa and Nairobi in July 2001, I made a case as to why the Kenyan Coast should be treated as a distinct society the way French-speaking Quebec is championed as a distinct society in Canada. Since then I have been to Ghana where Ashanti is treated as a distinct society in a different sense.

As mentioned earlier, in August 2001 I was in Ghana where I was graciously received by the Asantehene or King Tutu II (alias King Solomon of Ashanti) in his palace in Kumasi. I was also received by the then president of Ghana, President J. A. Kufuor at "State House" in Accra. For the first time in the history of postcolonial Ghana, the head of state of Ghana is a loyal subject of the King of Ashanti.

When I met President Kufuor I referred to the dilemmas of protocol when the head of state of the country was a subject of the king of one of the provinces. The head of state assured me that his paramount duty is as head of state of all Ghanaians regardless of ethnic or regional background. It was only in relation to some Ashanti ceremonies when he himself is before the Asantehene that the president has to bow to ancient traditions of Ashanti.

Just as Ghana has its first Ashanti president, will Kenya have its first Coastal president? On the contrary for at least the next election, a Coastal president is most unlikely, let alone a Muslim one. The redrawing of constituencies at the Coast, and the demographic penetration of the Coast by non-Coastal Kenyans, may result in de facto gerrymandering in what were previously Muslim constituencies. There may be fewer Muslims elected from the Coast in future decades.

But Coastal indigenous people of all faiths should not even think of ethnic cleansing as a solution to the new demographic realities. Coastal indigenes should counterbalance this de facto demographic gerrymandering with better political planning and more efficient coalition building. American Muslims are already cultivating allies among non-Muslim civil rights organizations and defenders of religious freedom, be they Christian, Jewish, or others. Kenyan Muslims and other Coastal Kenyans should also cultivate the skills of coalition building. Alliances between lovers of Kiswahili and those interested in Islam are one form of cultural coalition building.

Nobody in Malawi expected that Dr. Hastings Kamuzu Banda, Elder of the Church of Scotland, who had ruled the country for so long with an iron hand, would one day be defeated in an election by a Muslim—Dr. Bakali Muluzi. In Sierra Leone prolonged rule by non-Muslims finally resulted in chaos and war. Out of the chaos the country turned for the first time to a Muslim president—Ahmed Tejan Kabbah. Unfortunately the chaos and the war were too far-gone to be ended by a mere electoral change.

Kenya does not stand a chance of producing either a Coastal or a Muslim president in the near future—although each of Kenya's immediate neighbors (Tanzania, Uganda, Somalia, Sudan, and even Ethiopia—the five countries with which Kenya shares borders) has had a Muslim

head of state at some time or another. With planning and coalition building, a Muslim or Coastal vice president of Kenya is entirely in the cards.
After all, nobody during the days of either Kofi Busia or Kwame Nkrumah expected Ghana to produce a Muslim vice president. And yet it did
happen that Alhaji Aliu Mahama served as the vice president of Ghana
under the Kufuor administration.

In Kenya, just as the United States, it is not enough for Muslims to be
merely citizens; they must also be engaged in the affairs of their nation.
Nor is it enough for Muslims to be voters in elections; they should seek
public office and run for elections. They should have political targets and
specific goals.

African countries that are overwhelmingly Muslim have sometimes
permitted a non-Muslim to be their president. The percentage of Muslims
in Senegal is 94 percent in 2014—higher than the percentage of Muslims
in Egypt. Yet Senegal had a Roman Catholic president for twenty years—
Léopold Sédar Senghor. This open, African society, overwhelmingly
Muslim, could have a Christian president without cries of "JIHAD" in the
streets of Dakar at any stage over a period of twenty years (1960–1980).

The Muslim minority in Kenya is at least three times the size of the
Christian minority in Senegal in terms of percentages—and much more
numerous in absolute numbers than Christians in Senegal. If coalition
building in Senegal could produce a Christian president in an overwhelmingly Muslim country, coalition building in Kenya should produce
a Muslim vice president in the foreseeable future. A Muslim vice president for Kenya could of course be a Somali rather than a Coastal person.
That would also be a major step forward for the people of the Northeast
who have often been marginalized, if not victimized, by succeeding regimes. I would wholeheartedly support a qualified Somali vice president
of Kenya, but for the time being I would not support special autonomy
for the Northeast. That would lead to even greater neglect of the Somali
people and their deeper marginalization.

LANGUAGE POLICY AND NATIONAL INTEGRATION

We referred earlier to the scheme of electoral polygamy proposed by
Obote (one candidate, four constituencies). This scheme was bound to be
a major boost to the Swahili language in Uganda. If each prospective
Member of Parliament needed support in all the four corners of Uganda

(north-south-east-west), the system would have needed a lingua franca, a common language.

English was an appropriate lingua franca at the elite level, but quite inadequate in Uganda as a grassroots medium of discourse. Luganda and Kiswahili were the two rival grassroots interethnic languages. Obote's scheme of electoral polygamy would have dramatically enhanced the political fortunes of the Swahili language. Kiswahili is widely regarded as a detribalizing language. This is certainly true in Tanzania and Kenya. Kiswahili enables members of different tribes to communicate with each other and work together in trade unions, in political parties, as passengers on matatu,[13] and as participants in wider social affairs.

However, without Milton Obote's scheme of electoral polygamy, Kiswahili in Uganda has had both a nationalizing and a tribalizing role. Kiswahili's nationalizing credentials hinged on the fact that it was a grassroots language that was not tribe specific. That was in sharp contrast to Luganda, which could not but be associated with the largest ethnic group in Uganda, the Baganda.

But in Uganda Kiswahili has also had an ethnoregionalizing impact on the political process. Kiswahili has sometimes been regarded as a linguistic North-South divide—a language associated with Northerners and often resented by the largest group of Southerners, the Baganda. Since the British colonial period, Buganda has regarded Kiswahili as an objectionable rival to Luganda and has always wished Kiswahili would go away.

On the other hand, Northern Ugandans have often regarded it as their own intertribal lingual franca. Under British rule Kiswahili was the language of command in the King's African Rifles and in the Uganda police. The security forces in Uganda were disproportionately Northern.

In 1966, I was briefly in military custody in Kampala. The soldiers who were holding me did not know who I was and I thought ignorance of my identity was bliss on that occasion. All that the soldiers were interested in was to test my command of Kiswahili. If I failed completely I was going to be in serious trouble. On the other hand, I did not want my Kiswahili to sound too sophisticated in case it created in the soldiers a different kind of resentment. It was a delicate balancing act. I needed to pass the Swahili test, but I also had to avoid giving the soldiers a linguistic inferiority complex.

I witnessed before my distressed eyes what happened to those who failed the Swahili test. They were humiliated, literally made to lie on the floor and bite the dust, kicked around. It was petty but humiliating ethnic bullying of Southerners who could not speak Kiswahili. Kiswahili was a passport out of that ethnic humiliation. In the Uganda of the 1960s, Kiswahili was sometimes tribalizing rather than detribalizing.

In Kenya since the beginning of the twentieth century, on the other hand, Kiswahili has had a dramatic record as a language of national integration. From decade to decade it has become more and more widespread as a language of national discourse. But there have been anomalies. Kiswahili has been the language of practical politics but not the official language of the constitution. It has increasingly become the language of morals preached in churches and mosques, but not the language of the law in courts. It is the primary operational language of the head of state, but not of the chief justice.

The Kenyatta years had an additional paradox. The head of state (Kenyatta) was the most pro-Kiswahili member of the government. His most powerful minister in the 1970s (Charles Njonjo) was the most pro-English member of the government. Kenyatta went so far as to order Parliament to switch overnight to Kiswahili as the only language of legislative debate. Out of the blue, brilliant orators of English of yesterday became almost tongue-tied in Kiswahili today—and modest English speakers of last week promptly matured into Churchillian oratory in Kiswahili this week.

After Kenyatta's death there was an effort to have a parliamentary compromise with a bilingual parliament. In reality the pro-English forces were on the ascendancy in parliament. A future constitution should make this parliamentary bilingualism more real. It is not enough that members of Parliament should have the option to speak in either English or Kiswahili; Hansard, as the record of the parliamentary debates, should be bilingual in its entirety. Moreover, ministers in the government should be required to give at least one third of their major policy statements in each official language—Kiswahili and English—in the course of each parliamentary session. Language policy can thus be used as an important instrument of ethnic checks and balances.

In conclusion, this discussion began by distinguishing democracy as "ends" from democracy as "means." The same ends of democracy can be realized by different means. Africa should embrace the same ends (or goals) of democracy as the West—accountable rulers, freely participating citizens, an open society, and the pursuit of justice. But Africa should explore what democratic means would work for the continent in pursuing those goals.

Given that African political behavior is strongly susceptible to ethnic forces, African democratic means should take that paramount factor into account. And yet postcolonial African constitutions have tended to be in denial about ethnicity—often pretending that African states were ready-made nation-states qualified to be fully fledged unitary states.

Since ethnicity and its consequent realities will remain with Africa societies for at least another hundred years, political detribalization is not an option. We need ethnic checks and balances of a creative and constructive kind.

The constitution of Ethiopia after Mengistu Haile Mariam has attempted a federation of cultures and a theoretical system of ethnic balance. But in reality while the Oromo, for example, may be empowered at the regional level, they are not really empowered at the national level. The Ethiopian constitution has made progress in giving autonomy to the regions, but not enough progress in sharing power at the center. An equitable, ethnic partnership needs to do both—give more autonomy to the provinces and provide some genuine power sharing at the center.

In Ethiopia the war with Eritrea has not helped the constitutional experiment. Military mobilization tends to trample underfoot regional claims to autonomy.

This chapter posed the question, "If African politics are ethnic prone, can African constitutions be ethnic proof?" Surely not many in Kenya have needed much persuasion that African politics are indeed ethnic prone. We have drawn attention to some of the constitutional devices that were intended to be ethnic proof—the one-party state, the no-party state, the regionally rotating presidency, Milton Obote's electoral polygamy, the multiprovincial minimum for a presidential election. Some of these devices are still worth considering as potential ethnic checks and balances, while others (like the one-party state) have been discredited over most of Africa.

Let us hope Ethiopia and Eritrea rebuild their countries and find peace and greater cooperation. Kenya should shed the superstition that in order to foster national consciousness the country must be a unitary state. Both the Federal Republic of Germany and the United States are nationally conscious societies with a great propensity for patriotism and deep love of country. Yet neither Germany nor the United States are unitary states. They are indeed federations.

Local loyalties are perfectly compatible with national patriotism provided the whole system is inclusive and accommodates difference without marginalizing smaller groups. As a wise voice from Kisii has reminded fellow Kenyans:

> It is important to accept at this stage that the aspect of ethnicity is so entrenched in the country's politics that it is impossible to put the country together without a system of inclusive government. The first step towards this is to find a way of dealing with ethnicity from a positive perspective, and rehabilitate the national consciousness as a process of restructuring the country's political economy.[14]

But in Africa no ethnic checks and balances can endure unless women are also involved in a serious way. That is why we also need gender checks and balances. British colonialists may never forget Nana Yaa Asantewa, the warrior Queen Mother of Ashanti. Nor will Yoweri Museveni forget Alice Lakwena, the woman who led the Acholi to battle against Museveni. We do need to know more about the role of women in traditional political systems, and see what we can learn from these ancestral cultures.

But we know enough already about men and women to insist that the next Kenya constitution should more systematically defend, protect, and promote the participation of women in the political destiny of Kenya. The minimum of forty-seven women stipulated in the current constitution could be improved considering the male/female ratio in educational enrollment and among the entire Kenyan population. More women should be given ministerial or cabinet appointments. The Great Gold Coast philosopher Dr. Kwegyir Aggrey once said, "You can play a tune of a sort on the black keys of a piano. And you can play another tune of a sort on the white keys. But for real harmony you need both the black and the white keys" (Mazrui, 2014, p. 319).

Languages sometimes give genders to things. In Arabic the sun is feminine; the moon is masculine. What if the piano keys had gender in our language? What if the white keys were feminine and the black keys were masculine in some Kenyan language?

So far we have been able to play a tune of a sort with the masculine keys on the piano of Kenya politics. If women were in charge, we would be playing feminine keys on the piano of Kenyian politics. The tunes also have to do with taking stock of the overall nature and characteristic of a society and bringing them together to take advantage of the full potential of the society. For genuine historical harmony and great political symphony, let us make sure that both the feminine and the masculine keys are playing music together on Kenya's grand political piano.

NOTES

1. See chapter 7.
2. See Francis Wiafe-Amoako, *Human Security and Sierra Leone's Post-Conflict Development* (Lanham, MD: Lexington Books, 2014).
3. See Ricardo René Laremont and Fouad Kalouche, eds., *Africa and Other Civilizations: Conquest and Counter-Conquest* (Trenton, NJ: Africa World Press, 2002).
4. This obviously must be backed by a strong rule of law and a culture of deferring to the unflinching implementation of the rule of law and constitutional provisions
5. These are unwritten rules or norms. Among the Ashantis in Ghana, it is believed that it is the woman who knows the true father of her child. Thus assigning the queen mother the responsibility to appoint the powerful Ashanti king is a symbol that the legitimate king would be chosen.
6. This refers to a situation in which informal and unwritten norms and rules are entrenched within a society to such an extent that without formal leadership, the society is able to organize itself for stability and development.
7. Parliaments in Africa that have had a women speaker include South Africa, 1994; Ethiopia, 1995; Lesotho, 2000, Liberia, 2003; Burundi, 2005; Zimbabwe, 2005; Gambia, 2006 and 2009; Swaziland, 2006; Nigeria, 2007; Rwanda, 2008; Ghana, 2009; Botswana, 2009; Tanzania, 2010; Uganda, 2011; Equatorial Guinea, 2013; Madagascar, 2013; and Mauritius, 2014 ("Women Speakers of National Parliaments," Inter-Parliamentary Union, www.ipu.org/wmn-e/speakers.htm).
8. See the Taif Agreement; Section II (G) of the Taif Agreement abolished sectarianism at various institutions and in the workplace, and established the sharing of top-level jobs, which are to be shared equally between Christians and Muslims without allocating to any particular job to any sect.
9. This refers to political devolution of power within Kenya's society around the time of the country's independence. The idea was to create an ethnically based government that is autonomous in the European/white-settler region in Kenya.
10. See Wiafe-Amoako, *Human Security and Sierra Leone's Post-Conflict Development*, 2014.
11. Since 1999 when the Fourth Republic of Nigeria was ushered in, there have been successive elections without the interruption of military takeover of power.
12. The 1995 Constitution authorized the Movement as the only political organization in Uganda. Movement, chaired by Museveni, was described as not being a political party, but an umbrella under which all Ugandans should congregate.
13. These are privately owned minibuses that ply the streets of Nairobi, Kenya. There have been government regulations over the years to phase out these minibuses

in favor of bigger, commuting buses in Kenya. Very few matatus are currently in operation in Nairobi.

14. Simeon Nyachae EGH., MP, "An Inclusive and Accommodative Way Forward": The Case for a Government of National Unity in Kenya," paper published in Nairobi, May 2001.

Bibliography

Abraham, R. G. 1973. "Some Aspects of Levirate." In *The Character of Kinship*, edited by Jack Goody. Cambridge: Cambridge University Press, 163–74.

Adepoju, Aderanti, and Christine Oppong, eds. 1994. *Gender, Work and Population in Africa*. London: James Currey and Portsmouth, NH: Heinemann.

Ake, Claude. ed. 1985. "The State in Contemporary Africa." In *Political Economy of Nigeria*. London: Longman.

Ake, Claude. 1996. *Democracy and Development in Africa*. Washington, DC: Brookings Institution Press.

Allman, Jean, ed. 2004. *Fashioning Africa: Power and the Politics of Dress*. Bloomington: Indiana University Press.

Anderson, David. 2005. *Histories of the Hanged: The Dirty War in Kenya and the End of Empire*. New York: W. W. Norton.

Africans: A Triple Heritage, The. 1986. Great Britain: BBC-TV.

Ankomah, Baffour. 1998. "Bombers Hit Africa." *New African* 367 (October): 16–17.

Anonymous. 2004. *Imperial Hubris: Why the West Is Losing the War on Terror*. Washington, DC: Brassey's, 55–67.

Apraku, Kofi A. 1991. *African Emigres in the United States: A Missing Link in Africa's Social and Political Development*. New York: Praeger.

Arendt, Hannah. 1972. *Crisis of the Republic*. New York: Harcourt Brace Jovanovich.

Arthur, John A. 2000. *Invisible Sojourners: African Immigrant Diaspora in the United States* Westport, CT: Praeger.

Associated Press. 2001. *Hamilton Spectator*, November 24, p. D2.

Atieno-Odhiambo, E. S. 1997. *Jaramogi Ajuma Oginga Odinga*. Nairobi: East African Educational Publishers.

Avella, Steven M., and Elizabeth McKeown, eds. 1999. *Public Voices: Catholics in the American Context*. Maryknoll, NY: Orbis Books.

Ayittey, G. 2006. "The Native System of Government: A Summary and an Assessment." In *Indigenous African Institutions*, 2nd ed. New York: Transnational Publishers, 265–310.

Bhagwati, Jagdish. 2004. *In Defense of Globalization*. New York: Oxford University Press.

Bamikole, Lawrence O. 2012. "Nkrumah and the Triple Heritage Thesis and Development." *Africana Studies in International Journal of Business, Humanities and Technology* 2 (2): 68–76.

Bamyeh, Mohammed A. 2000. *The Ends of Globalization*. Minneapolis: University of Minnesota Press.

Barber, Benjamin. 1995. *Jihad vs. McWorld*. New York: Times Books.

Barley, S., and Tolbert, P. 1997. "Institutionalization and Structuration: Studying the Links between Action and Institution." *Organization Studies* 18 (1, January): pp. 93–117.

Barre, Mohamed Siad. 1976. "Revolutionary Resolve." *World Marxist Review* 19 (5): 26.

Bayart, J. F. 1993. "Introduction: The Historicity of the African State." In *The State in Africa: The Politics of the Belly*. London: Longman.

Bayne, Nicholas. 2000. "Why Did Seattle Fail? Globalization and the Politics of Trade." *Government and Opposition* 35 (2, Spring): 131–51.

Béjar, Alejandro Álvarez. 2007. "Mexico after the Elections: The Crisis of Legitimacy and the Exhaustion of Predatory Liberalism." *Monthly Review—An Independent Socialist Magazine* 59 (3, July–August). http://monthlyreview.org/2007/07/01/mexico-after-the-elections-the-crisis-of-legitimacy-the-exhaustion-of-predatory-neoliberalism/. Accessed: December 7, 2014.

Bell, Daniel. 1960. *The End of Ideology*. Glencoe: Illinois Press.

Bell, M. J. V. 1965. *Army and Nation in Sub-Saharan Africa*. London: International Institute for Strategic Studies.

Bhagwati, Jagdish. 2004. *In Defense of Globalization*. New York: Oxford University Press.

Birch, Anthony H. 2001. *The Concepts and Theories of Modern Democracy*. 2nd ed. London and New York: Routledge.

Blight, James G., and David A. Welch, 1989. *On the Brink: Americans and Soviets Reexamine the Cuban Missile Crisis*. New York: Hill and Wang.

Bogle, Lori L., ed. 2001. *The Cold War*. New York: Routledge.

Bohnet, I., and Baytelman, Y. 2007. "Institutions and Trust Implications for Preferences, Beliefs and Behavior." *Rationality and Society* 19 (1): 99–135.

Bridgewater, Pamela E. 2003. "The African Diaspora and Its Influence on African Development," speech delivered at Kentucky State University, March 28. http://usembassy-australia.state.gov/hyper/2003/0403/epf410.htm. Accessed March 24, 2004.

Brodber, Erna. 2003. *The Continent of Black Consciousness: On the History of the African Diaspora from Slavery to the Present Day*. London: New Beacon Books.

Broder, David. 2004. "Democrats Focus on Healing Divisions: Addressing Convention, Newcomers Set Themes." *The Washington Post*, July 28.

Brown Sherman, Mary A. 1993. *Building Consensus for Higher Education Reform in Africa: Some Reflections*. Washington, DC: World Bank.

Burke, Edmund. 2001. *Reflections on the Revolution in France: A Critical Edition*. Edited by J. C. D. Clarke. Stanford, CA: Stanford University Press.

Bute, E. L., and H. J. P. Harmer. 1997. *The Black Handbook: The People, History and Politics of Africa and the African Diaspora*. London and Washington, DC: Cassell.

Casimiro, Isabel. 1986. "Transformação nas Relações Homem/Mulher em Moçambique 1960-74" [Changing Gender Relations in Mozambique, 1964-74]. Licenciatura, Universidade Eduardo Mondlane, Maputo.

Casimiro, Isabel. 1999. "Peace in the Country, War at Home. Feminism and Women Organization in Mozambique, 1987-97." MA, Sociology, Universidade de Coimbra, Coimbra, Portugal.

Chazan, Naomi, et al. 1992. *Politics and Societies in Contemporary Africa*. 2nd ed. Boulder, CO: Lynne Reinner Publishers.

Clough, Marshall S. 1998. *Mau Mau Memoirs: History, Memory, and Politics*. Boulder, CO: Lynne Reinner Publishers.

Coleman, Christopher B. 1914. *Constantine the Great and Christianity, Three Phases: The Historical, the Legendary, and the Spurious*. New York: Columbia University Press.

Collier-Thomas, Bettye, and V. P. Franklin. 2001. *Sisters in the Struggle: African American Women in the Civil Rights–Black Power Movements*. New York: New York University Press.

Conniff, Michael L., and Thomas J. Davis. 1994. *Africans in the Americas: A History of the Black Diaspora*. New York: St. Martin's Press.

Coram, B. T. 1996. "Second Best Theories and the Implications for Institutional Design." In *The Theory of Institutional Design*, edited by Robert E. Goodin. New York: Cambridge University Press.

Cutrufelli, Maria Rosa. 1983. *Women of Africa: Roots of Oppression*. London: Zed Press.

Davidson, B. 1992. "The Black Man's Burden." In *The Black Man's Burden: Africa and the Curse of the Nation-State*. New York: Times Books, 194–243.

Deringil, Selim. 1993. "The Invention of Tradition as Public Image in the Late Ottoman Empire, 1808 to 1908." *Comparative Studies in Society and History* 35 (1): 3–29.

Deutsch, K. and William Foltz. 1966. *Nation-Building*. New York: Atherton Press.

Diamond, Larry, Juan Linz, and Seymour Martin Lipset, eds. 1988. *Democracy in Developing Countries*. Vol. 2. Boulder, CO: Lynne Reinner Publishers.

Dryzek, J. 1996. "The Informal Logic of Institutional Design." In *The Theory of Institutional Design*, edited by Robert E. Goodin. New York: Cambridge University Press.

Elkins, Caroline. 2005. *Imperial Reckoning: The Untold Story of Britain's Gulag in Kenya*. New York: Henry Holt.

Engels, Frederick. 1880. *Socialism: Utopian and Scientific*. Moscow: Progress Publishers [1970].

Esedebe, P. Olisanwuche. 1994. *Pan-Africanism: The Idea and Movement, 1776–1991*. 2nd ed. Washington, DC: Howard University.

Eubank, Keith. 2000. *The Missile Crisis in Cuba*. Malabar, FL: Krieger Publishing Company.

Falola, Toyin. 2003. *The Power of African Cultures*. Rochester, NY: University of Rochester Press.

Fanon, Frantz. 1963. *The Wretched of the Earth*. Trans. Constance Farrington. New York: Grove Press.

Feldman, David. 1993. *Civil Liberties and Human Rights in England and Wales*. Oxford, UK: Clarendon Press; New York: Oxford University Press.

First, Ruth. 1970. *The Barrel of a Gun: Political Power in Africa and the Coup*. London: Allen Lane.

Foltz, William J. 1983. "The Organization of African Trouble: How and Why It Works and Does Not Work." *Report 689-AR, US Department of State*, Mimeograph, September, p. 18.

Friedrichs, David. 1980. "The Legitimacy Crisis in the United States: A Conceptual Analysis." *Social Problems* 27 (5): 540–55.

Gavin, Francis J., ed. 2001. *The Cold War*. Chicago: Fitzroy Dearborn Publishers.

Gendzier, Irene. 1985. *Managing Political Change: Social Scientist and the Third World*. Boulder, CO: Westview Press.

Ghosh, B. N. 2001. *Contemporary Issues in Development Economics*. London and New York: Routledge.

Goldsworthy, David. 1982. *Tom Mboya: The Man Kenya Wanted to Forget*. New York: Africana Publishing Company.

Gordon, April. 1998. "The New Diaspora: African Immigration to the United States." *Journal of Third World Studies* 15 (Spring): 79–103.

Gunaratna, Rohan. 2002. *Inside Al Qaeda: Global Network of Terror*. London: Hurst & Co.

Habermas, Jürgen. 1975. *Legitimacy Crisis*. Boston: Beacon Press.

Halpern, Manfred. 1962. "Middle Eastern Armies and the New Middle Class." In *The Role of the Military in the Underdeveloped Countries*, edited by J. J. Johnson. Princeton, NJ: Princeton University Press.

Halpern, Manfred. 1963. *The Politics of Social Change in the Middle East and North Africa*. Princeton, NJ: Princeton University Press.

Hardin, R. 1996. "Institutional Morality." In *The Theory of Institutional Design*, edited by Robert E. Goodin. New York: Cambridge University Press.

Harris, Joseph E., ed. 2003. *Global Dimensions of the African Diaspora*. 2nd ed. Washington, DC: Howard University Press.

Hay, Margaret Jean. 1976. "Luo Women and Economic Change during the Colonial Period." In *Women in Africa: Studies in Social and Economic Change*, edited by Nancy J. Hafkin and Edna G. Bay. Stanford, CA: Stanford University Press, 87–110.

Hayami, Yujiro. 2001. *Development Economics: From the Poverty to the Wealth of Nations*. Oxford and New York: Oxford University Press.

Haynes, Jeff, ed. 2000. *Religion, Globalization and Political Culture in the Third World*. New York: St. Martin's Press.

Hays, Colin, and David Marsh, eds. 2000. *Demystifying Globalization*. New York: St. Martin's Press in association with Polsis, University of Birmingham.

Henisz, Witold. 2004. "Political Institution and Policy Volatility." *Economics and Politics* 16 (1): 1–27.

Hensley, Thomas R. ed. 2001. *The Boundaries of Freedom of Expression & Order in American Democracy*. Kent, OH: Kent State University Press.

Herbst, Jeffrey. 2000. *States and Power in Africa*. Princeton, NJ: Princeton University Press.

Hine, Darlene Clark, and Jacqueline McLeod, eds. 1999. *Crossing Boundaries: Comparative History of Black People in Diaspora*. Bloomington: Indiana University Press.

Hobbes, Thomas. [1668] 1996. *Leviathan*. Oxford: Oxford University Press.

Hodgson, D. 2006. "What Are Institutions?" *Journal of Economic Issues* 40 (1): 1–21.

Hope, Sr., Kempe Ronald, and Bornwell C. Chikulo, eds. 2000. *Corruption and Development in Africa: Lessons from Country Case Studies*. New York: St. Martin's Press.

Horowitz, Irving Louis. 1966. *Three Worlds of Development*. New York: Oxford University Press.

Huntington, Samuel. 1971. "The Change to Change: Modernization, Development, and Politics." *Comparative Politics* 3 (3): 55–79.

Hunwick, John, and Eve T. Powell. 2002. *The African Diaspora in the Mediterranean Lands of Islam*. Princeton, NJ: Markus Wiener Publishers.

Iheduru, Obioma M., ed. 2001. *Contending Issues in African Development: Advances, Challenges, and the Future*. Westport, CT: Greenwood Press.

Ihonvbere, Julius O. 1994. "The 'Irrelevant' State, Ethnicity, and the Quest for Nationhood in Africa." *Ethnic and Racial Studies* 17 (January): 42–60.

Ihonvbere, Julius O. 1997. "On the Threshold of Another False Start? A Critical Evaluation of Prodemocracy Movements in Africa." In *Democracy and Democratization in Africa: Toward the 21st Century*, edited by E. Ike Udogu. New York: E. J. Brill, 125–42.

Iliffe, John. 1993. "The Organization of the Maji Maji Rebellion." In *Conquest and Resistance to Colonialism in Africa*, edited by Gregory Maddox. New York: Garland.

Inikori, Joseph E., and Stanley L. Engerman, eds. 1992. *The Atlantic Slave Trade: Effects on Economies and Peoples in Africa, the Americas, and Europe*. Durham, NC: Duke University Press.

Jalloh, Alusine, and Stephen E. Maizlish, eds. 1996. *The African Diaspora*. College Station: Texas A&M University Press.

Jayasuriya, Shihan De Silva, and Richard Pankhurst, eds. 2003. *T he African Diaspora in the Indian Ocean*. Trenton, NJ: Africa World Press.

Kamau, John. 2004. "How Kenya's Best Kept Secret Became a Hotbed of Insurgents." *Sunday Standard* (Nairobi), July 11.

Kant, Immanual. 1795. "Perpetual Peace: A Philosophical Sketch."

Keller, Edmond J., and Barbara Thomas-Woolley. 1994. "Majority Rules and Minority Rights: American Federalism and African Experience." *Journal of Modern African Studies* 32 (3): 411–27.

Kimenyi, Mwangi S. 1998. "Harmonizing Ethnic Claims in Africa: A Proposal for Ethnic-Based Federalism." *CATO Journal* 18 (1): 43–64.

Kinsley, Michael. 2002. "Listening to Our Inner Ashcrofts." *Washington Post*, January 4, p. 27.

Kiros, Teodros. 2001. *Explorations in African Political Thought: Identity, Community, Ethics*. New York: Routledge.

Konvitz, Milton R. 2001. *Fundamental Rights: History of a Constitutional Doctrine*. New Brunswick, NJ: Transaction Publishers/Rutgers University.

Kuofir, Nelson. 1998. "No-Party Democracy in Uganda." *Journal of Democracy* 9 (2): 49–63.

Kyle, Keith. 1999. *The Politics of the Independence of Kenya*. New York: St. Martin's Press in association with Institute of Contemporary British History.

Laïdi, Zaki. 1990. *The Superpowers and Africa: The Constraints of a Rivalry, 1960–1990*. Chicago: University of Chicago Press.

Laremont, Ricardo René, and Fouad Kalouche, eds. 2002. *Africa and Other Civilizations: Conquest and Counter-Conquest*. Trenton, NJ: Africa World Press.

Lasswell, Harold. 1936. *Politics: Who Gets What, When, How*. New York: Whittlesey House.

Le Carré, John. 1964. *The Spy Who Came In from the Cold*. New York: Coward-McCann.

Luban, D. 1996. "The Publicity Principle." In *The Theory of Institutional Design*, edited by Robert E. Goodin. New York: Cambridge University Press.

Machel, Samora. 1980. "Le Processus de la Revolution Democratique Populaire au Mozambique." *Canadian Journal of African Studies* 14(2): 361–363.

Malcomson, Scott L. 2004. "An Appeal beyond Race." *The New York Times*, August 1.

Maloba, Wunyabari. 1993. *Mau Mau and Kenya: An Analysis of a Peasant Revolt*. Bloomington: Indiana University Press.

Mannheim, Karl. 1960. *Ideology and Utopia*. London: Routledge and Kegan Paul.

Marable, Manning. 1989. *Black Leadership*. New York: Columbia University Press.

Marshall, P. J., ed. 2001. *The Cambridge Illustrated History of the British Empire*. New York: Cambridge University Press.

Marte, Fred. 1994. *Political Cycles in International Relations: The Cold War and Africa, 1945–1990*. Amsterdam: VU University Press.

Martin, Guy. 2012. *African Political Thought*. New York: Palgrave Macmillan.

Mazrui, Al-Amin Bin Ali. 1995. *The History of the Mazru'i Dynasty of Mombasa*. Edited by J. M. Ritchie. Oxford: Oxford University Press.

Mazrui, Ali A. 1986. *The Africans: A Triple Heritage*. Boston: Little, Brown.

Mazrui, Ali A., ed. 1993. *General History of Africa*. Vol 8, *Africa since 1935*. Paris: UNESCO.

Mazrui, Ali A. 2002. "The Frankenstein State and the Internal Order." In *Africa and Other Civilizations: Conquest and Counter-Conquest*, edited by René Ricardo Laremont and Fouad Kalouche. Trenton, NJ: Africa World Press, 303–29.

Mazrui, Ali A. 2006. *A Tale of Two Africans: Nigeria and South Africa as Contrasting Visions*. Edited by James N. Karioki. London: Adonis and Abbey Publishers.

Mazrui, Ali A. 2014. *African Thought in Comparative Perspective*. Edited by Ramzi Badran, Seifudein Adem, and Patrick Dikirr. Newscastle: Cambridge Scholars Publishing

Mbaku, John. 1996. "Effective Constitutional Discourse as an Important First Step to Democratization in Africa." *Journal of Asian and African Studies* 31 (June): 39–51.

McLuhan, Marshall, and Bruce R. Powers. 1989. *The Global Village: Transformations in World Life and Media in the 21st Century*. New York: Oxford University Press.

Mill, John Stuart. [1859] 1978. *On Liberty*. Indianapolis, IN: Hackett Publishing Company.

Ministry of Information and Broadcasting. 1979. *Collected Works of Mahatma Gandhi*. Vol. 77. New Delhi and Ahmedabad: Government of India and the Navajivan Trust.

Mookherjee, Dilip, and Debraj Ray, eds. 2001. *Readings in the Theory of Economic Development*. Malden, MA: Blackwell Publishers.

Mungazi, Dickson A., and L. K. Walker. 1997. *Educational Reform and the Transformation of Southern Africa*. Westport, CT: Praeger.

Munslow, Barry, ed. 1986. *Africa: Problems in the Transition to Socialism*. London: Zed Press.

Mwaura, Ndirangu. 2005. *Kenya Today: Breaking the Yoke of Colonialism in Africa*. New York: Algora Publishing.

Nascimento, Abdias do. 2005. "Blacks and Politics in Brazil." In *Africana: The Encyclopedia of the African and African American Experience*, 2nd ed., edited by Kwame Anthony Appiah and Henry Louis Gates, Jr., 1: p. 619. Oxford and New York: Oxford University Press.

National Commission on Terrorist Attacks upon the United States. 2004. *9/11 Commission Report: Final Report of the National Commission on Terrorist Attacks upon the United States*. New York: W. W. Norton.

Ndubuike, Darlington I. I. 2002. *The Struggles, Challenges and Triumphs of the African Immigrant in America*, Lewiston, NY: Edwin Mellen Press.

Neale, W. 1987. "Institutions." *Journal of Economic Issues* 21 (3): 1178–1202.

Nkrumah, Kwame. 1962. *Towards Colonial Freedom: Africa in the Struggle against World Imperialism*. London: Heinemann.

Nkrumah, Kwame. 1964. *Consciencism: Philosophy and Ideology for Decolonization*. London: Heinemann.

North, Douglas. 1991. "Institutions." *Journal of Economic Perspective* 5 (1): 77–112.

"Now for Africa." 2003. *The Economist*, July 5.

Nyachae, Simeon EGH, MP. 2001. "An Inclusive and Accommodative Way Forward": The Case for a Government of National Unity in Kenya." Paper published in Nairobi, May.

Nyerere, Julius K. 1960. "Africa's Place in the World." In Wellesley College *Symposium on Africa*. Wellesley, MA.

Nyerere, Julius K. 1961. "Spearhead." Reprinted in *The Ideologies of the Developing Nations*, edited by Paul E. Sigmund. New York: Praeger, 1963.

Nyerere, Julius K. 1966. *Freedom and Unity*. London: Oxford University Press.

Odinga, Oginga. 1968. *Not Yet Uhuru: The Autobiography of Oginga Odinga*. Portsmouth, ME: Heinemann.

Offe, C. 1996. "Designing Institutions in East European Transitions." In *The Theory of Institutional Design*, edited by Robert E. Goodin. New York: Cambridge University Press, 199–227.

Ogot, B. A., and W. R. Ochieng', eds. 1995. *Decolonization and Independence in Kenya*. London: James Currey; Athens, OH: University Press, 1995.

Oruka, H. Odera, ed. 1992. *Oginga Odinga: His Philosophy and Beliefs*. Nairobi: Initiatives Publishers.

Osabu-Kle, Daniel T. 2000. *Compatible Cultural Democracy: The Key to Development in Africa*. Peterborough, ON; Orchard Park, NY: Broadview Press.

Ottaway, Marina and David. In *Afrocommunism*. Teaneck, NJ: Holmes and Meier Publishers, Inc.

Ould-Mey, M. 1996. "Democratization in Africa: The Political Face of SAPS." *Journal of Third World Studies* 12 (2): 122–58.

Palmer, Monte. 1989. *Dilemmas of Political Development: An Introduction to the Politics of the Developing Areas*. Itasca, IL: F. E. Peacock Publishers.

p'Bitek, Okot. 1971. *African Religions in Western Scholarship*. Nairobi: East African Literature Bureau.

Pear, Robert. 2005. "Racial and Ethnic Minorities Gain in the Nation as a Whole." *The New York Times*, August 12.

Peters, Guy. 2012. *African Political Thought*. New York: Palgrave.

Pettit, P. 1996. "Institutional Design and Rational Choice." In *The Theory of Institutional Design*, edited by Robert E. Goodin. New York: Cambridge University Press, 54–90.

Popper, Karl. 1991. *The Poverty of Historicism*, New York: Routledge.

Prestowitz, Clyde. 2005. *Three Billion New Capitalists: The Great Shift of Wealth and Power to the East*. New York: Basic Books.

Przeworski, A. 2009. "Constraints and Choices: Electoral Participation in Historical Perspective." *Comparative Political Studies* 42 (1): 4–30.

Putnam, Robert D. 1973. *The Beliefs of Politicians*. New Haven, CT: Yale University Press.

Ranchod-Nilsson, Sita. 2006. "Gender Politics and the Pendulum of Political and Social Transformation in Zimbabwe." *Journal of Southern African Studies* 32 (1): 49-67.

Ranger, T. O. 1968. "Connexions between 'Primary Resistance' and Modern Nationalism in East and Central Africa, Parts I and II." *Journal of African History* 9 (4): 437–53 and 631–41.

Rawls, John. 1993. *Political Liberalism*. New York: Columbia University Press.

Raz, Joseph. 1986. *The Morality of Freedom*. Oxford: Oxford University Press.

Redmond, Patrick M. "Maji Maji in Ungoni: A Reappraisal of Existing Historiography." In *Conquest and Resistance to Colonialism in Africa*, edited by Gregory Maddox. New York: Garland.

Reus-Smit, Christian. 2007. "International Crises of Legitimacy." *International Politics* (44): 157–74.

Rich, V. 1992. "Africa's 'New Wind of Change,'" *World Today* 48 (7): 116–19.

Richards, Paul. 1996. *Fighting in the Rain Forest: War, Youth and Resources in Sierra Leone*. Oxford: James Currey.

Rupert, Mark. 2000. *Ideologies of Globalization: Contending Visions of a New World Order*. London and New York: Routledge.

Schatzberg, Michael G. 1993. "Power, Legitimacy and 'Democratization' in Africa." *Africa: Journal of the International African Institute* 63 (4): 445–61.

Scobie, Edward. 1994. *Global African Presence*. Brooklyn, NY: A & B Books.

Sethi, Patricia J. 1984. "We Have to Depend on Ourselves," interview of Thomas Sankara. *Newsweek*, November 19.

Shanda Tonme, Jean-Claude. 2005. "All Rock, No Action." *The New York Times*, July 15.

Shepsle, K. 1996. "Political Deals in Institutional Settings." In *The Theory of Institutional Design*, edited by Robert E. Goodin. New York: Cambridge University Press, 227–40

Silberschmidt, M. 1991. *Rethinking Men and Gender Relations: An Investigation of Men, Their Changing Roles within the Household, and the Implications for Gender Relations in Kisii District, Kenya*. Copenhagen: Center for Development Research.

Sindima, Harvey J. 1995. *Africa's Agenda: The Legacy of Liberalism and Colonialism in the Crisis of African Values*. Westport, CT: Greenwood Press.

Stiglitz, Joseph E. 2003. *Globalization and Its Discontents*. New York: W. W. Norton.

Storey, John W., and Glenn H. Utter. 2002. *Religion and Politics: A Reference Handbook*. Santa Barbara, CA: ABC-CLIO.

Stromberg, Roland N. 1996. *Democracy: A Short, Analytical History*. Armonk, NY: M. E. Sharpe.

Suberu, Rotimi T. 2001. *Federalism and Ethnic Conflict in Nigeria*. Washington, DC: United States Institute of Peace Press.

Suberu, Rotimi T. 2004. "Nigeria: Dilemmas of Federalism." In *Federalism and Territorial Cleavages*, edited by Ugo M. Amoretti and Nancy Bermeo. Baltimore, MD: Johns Hopkins University Press, 327–54.

Suchman, M. C. 1995. "Managing Legitimacy: Strategic and Institutional Approaches." *Academy of Management Journal* 20 (3): 571–610.

Sullivan, Kevin. 2005. "Attempted Murder Charges Brought in London Attack." *The Washington Post*, August 9.

Tesfamichael, Gebreselassie Y. 2005. "In Africa, Just Help Us to Help Ourselves." *The Washington Post*, July 24.

Thomas, Darryl C. 2001. *The Theory and Practice of Third World Solidarity*. Westport, CT: Praeger.

Tordoff, William. 1993. *Government and Politics in Africa*. 2nd ed. Indianapolis: Indiana University Press.

Tripp, Alli M., Isabel Casimiro, Joy Kwesiga, and Alice Mungwa. 2009. *African Women's Movements: Changing Political Landscape*. New York: Cambridge University Press.

Tronvoll, Kjetil. 2000. *Ethiopia: A New Start?* London: Minority Rights Group.

Tsebelis, George. 2002. *Veto Player: How Political Institutions Work*. Princeton, NJ: Princeton University Press.

Udogu, E. Ike. 1999. "The Issue of Ethnicity and Democratization in Africa: Toward the Millennium." *Journal of Black Studies* 29 (6): 790–808.

United Nations Security Council (SC). 2000. Resolution 1325 (2000). October 31. http://www.un.org/womenwatch/ods/S-RES-1325(2000)-E.pdf.

Urdang, Stephanie. 1978. "Precondition for Victory': Women's Liberation in Mozambique and Guinea-Bissau," *Journal of Opinion* 8 (A1): 25–31.

van Heerde, Jennifer, Martin Johnson, and Shaun Bowler. 2006. "Barriers to Participation, Voter Sophistication and Candidate Spending in US Senate Elections." *British Journal of Political Science* 36 (4): 745–58.

Waswo, Ann. 1996. *Modern Japanese Society*. Oxford: Oxford University Press.

Weber, Max. 1964. *The Theory of Social and Economic Organizations*. Edited by Talcott Parsons. New York: Free Press.

Weingast, Barry. 1989. "Floor Behavior in the U.S. Congress: Committee Power under the Open Rule." *American Political Science Review* 83 (3), 795–815.

Wiafe-Amoako, Francis. 2014. *Human Security and Sierra Leone's Post-Conflict Development*. Lanham, MD: Lexington Books.

Williams, Michael W. 1992. *Pan-Africanism: An Annotated Bibliography*. Pasadena, CA: Salem Press.

"Women Speakers of National Parliaments." Inter-Parliamentary Union. www.ipu.org/wmn-e/speakers.htm.

Young, Crawford. 1982. *Ideology and Development in Africa*. New Haven, CT: Yale University Press.

Young, Crawford. 1990/1991. "Africa's Heritage of Colonialism." *TransAfrica Forum* 7 (4, Winter): p. 3.

Young, Crawford M. 2008. "The Heritage of Colonialism." In John W. Harbeson and Donald Rothchild, eds., *Africa in World Politics: Reforming Political Order*. Boulder, CO: Westview Press

Zelditch, Jr., Morris. (2001). "Theories of Legitimacy." In *The Psychology of Legitimacy: Emerging Perspectives on Ideology, Justice, and Intergroup Relations*, edited by John Jost and Brenda Major. Cambridge: Cambridge University Press, 33–53.

Zeng, Benxiang. 2014. "Women Political Participation in China: Improved or Not." *Journal of International Women's Studies* 15 (1): 136–50.

Index

ACCORD. *See* African Centre for the Constructive Resolution of Disputes

Africa,. *See also* South Africa 7, 20, 135; black-skinned leadership in, 77; civilizations of, 126; colonialism rooted out in, 43; constitution of, 19, 24–25; contemporary ideology in, 48–49; democracide in, 22–26; democracy in, 14, 17, 31, 33, 147; election periods dangerous in, 90–91; elites and army coup in, 23; European colonization of, 121; French, 22; gender's role in, 14–15; indigenous language of, 120–121; institutional legitimacy in, 81; Iron Law of Ethnicity in, 148; liberation movements of, 118; multiparty systems and, 93–94; nationalism in, 43–45, 76, 79; petroleum resources of, 98; populist socialism in, 45–47; postcolonial, 27–28; postindependence coup in, 83; regime types in, 65; religions role in, 126; scientific socialism in, 47–48; single-party system in, 116–117; stability and development of, 7–8; sub-Saharan, 149; unitary government system in, 122–123; vertical counterpenetration in, 132; wars of liberation in, 56; Western culture in, 21, 22; women and, 62, 65–66; women's organizations in, 66–67

African Americans, 142n33

African apparel, 119

African Centre for the Constructive Resolution of Disputes (ACCORD), 70

African Diaspora, 128, 136

African National Congress (ANC), 28

The Africans: A Triple Heritage (television), 146

African societies, 54–57, 56, 89, 91, 92–93

African states, 75–76, 77, 83–84, 101

African Union (AU), 3, 83

African Union Border Program (AUBP), 75, 97–98

African Union Mission in Somalia (AMISOM), 3

African Women Mediators Seminar, 70

Afrikaans Resistance Movement (AWB), 82

Afro-Asian solidarity movement, 129

Aggrey, Kwegyir, 160

agriculture, 44, 58

Aisha, Muhammad, 107

Ake, Claude, 3, 48

Algeria, 28, 62, 66, 105

Amin, Idi, 28, 103, 108, 148, 153

AMISOM. *See* African Union Mission in Somalia

ammunition ban, 9

ANC. *See* African National Congress

androgynous entrepreneurship, 61

Angola, 23, 26, 62, 84

apartheid, 55, 81, 100, 101

Aquino, Corazon, 28

Arab Spring, 111n4

Arap Moi, Daniel, 27, 30, 108, 116, 119

army coup, 23

Asantewa, Nana Yaa, 160

Ashanti kingdom, 91

Ashanti society, 150

Ashcroft, John, 31

assassinations, 113–114

Atlantic Alliance, 24

AU. *See* African Union

AUBP. *See* African Union Border Program

About the Authors

Professor Ali A. Mazrui obtained his doctoral degree from Oxford University in England and his excellent accomplishments in political science and African studies were remarkable. He was the Albert Schweitzer Professor in the Humanities and Director of the Institute of Global Cultural Studies at Binghamton University, State University of New York. He was also Albert Luthuli Professor-at-Large at the University of Jos in Nigeria. In addition, Mazrui was the Andrew D. White Professor-at-Large Emeritus and Senior Scholar in Africana Studies at Cornell University. Dr Mazrui also served as Chancellor of the Jomo Kenyatta University of Agriculture and Technology in Kenya—an appointment made by Kenya's head of state.

Professor Mazrui was a renowned teacher and scholar, had published hundreds of articles in five continents, and had been a speaker at several international conferences. An evaluation of Dr. Mazrui's scholarly contribution by other scholars is published in the book *Public Intellectuals in the Politics of Global Africa* (London, 2011), edited by Dr. Seifudein Adem. Dr. Mazrui's television work includes the widely discussed 1986 series *The Africans: A Triple Heritage* (BBC and PBS). A book by the same title was jointly published by BBC Publications and Little, Brown and Company. In 1986 the book was a best seller in Britain and was adopted or recommended by various book clubs in the United States, including the Book of the Month Club.

Professor Mazrui passed away in October 2014.

Dr. Francis Wiafe-Amoako holds a master of arts degree in political science from East Stroudsburg University in Pennsylvania, and another master of arts degree in political science with concentrations in international relations and comparative politics from Binghamton University. His passion for the politics, economics, and society of Africa led to him pursuing and obtaining a PhD in African studies from Howard University in Washington, D.C. Dr. Wiafe-Amoako's teaching career has spanned the fields of international relations and security, international development, peace negotiations, comparative political institutions, and politics of the global South. He has taught at the University of Toronto and Ryerson University in Canada, Samford University in Birmingham, Alabama; and Montgomery College in Rockville, Maryland; and was a visiting professor at the College of Wooster in Ohio.

Dr. Wiafe-Amoako's research focuses on migration and security, conflict management, post-conflict reconstruction, and institutional design in Africa. In 2014 Dr. Wiafe-Amoako's book, *Human Security and Sierra Leone's Post-Conflict Development* was published by Lexington Books (an imprint of Rowman & Littlefield). He is also the Director of the Center for Sustained Domestic Security and Development, whose main goal is the development of viable institutions in the developing world. Dr. Wiafe-Amoako is a consultant and a resource person leading short management training courses for senior and middle level public officials. Dr. Wiafe-Amoako is the current editor/author for "Africa," the World Today Series, an annual publication of historical and contemporary issues on the continent of Africa.